OUR WORLD GIS EDUCATION

Thinking Spatially Using GIS

ISBN-13: 9781589481800
Suggested
grade level: 3–6

Thinking Spatially Using GIS presents engaging lessons that use fundamental spatial concepts and introduce GIS software to young students. Students are guided to find relative and absolute locations of map features, create maps, locate human and physical features on maps, discover and analyze geographic distribution patterns, and investigate changes over time. *Thinking Spatially Using GIS* provides a platform to tie in conventional 3–6 grade level topics, including lessons learned on world and U.S. geography, world exploration, and demographics.

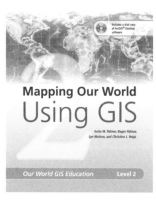

Mapping Our World Using GIS

ISBN-13: 9781589481817
Suggested
grade level: 6 and up

Mapping Our World Using GIS invites middle and high school students to investigate GIS through lessons that require critical thinking and problem-solving skills. These lessons align with national teaching standards for geography, science, and technology in introducing and building skills in geographic inquiry, spatial thinking, and GIS. Topics covered include studying landforms, physical processes, ecosystems, climate, vegetation, population patterns and processes, human and political geography, and human and environment interaction.

Analyzing Our World Using GIS

ISBN-13: 9781589481824
Suggested
grade level: 9 and up

In *Analyzing Our World Using GIS,* students gain proficiency working with GIS and exploring geographic data. High school and college students will complete sophisticated workflows such as downloading and editing data and analyzing patterns on maps. Topics covered include analyzing economics by exploring education funding, demographics, and trade alliances; analyzing land and ocean effects on climate; and plate tectonics analysis to describe earthquake and volcanic activity.

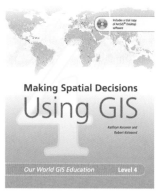

Making Spatial Decisions Using GIS

ISBN-13: 9781589481831
Suggested
grade level: 13 and up

Making Spatial Decisions Using GIS is intended for advanced high school, college, university, and technical school students. The book presents a wide variety of real-world settings for GIS analysis and decision making. Students learn methods for planning and executing GIS projects for more involved group investigations and independent study. Topics covered include analyzing hazardous emergency situations, using demographic data for analysis of population growth and urbanization trends, and using GIS to create reliable location intelligence that results in sound decisions.

Making Spatial Decisions
Using GIS

Kathryn Keranen
Robert Kolvoord

ESRI PRESS
REDLANDS, CALIFORNIA

Ask for ESRI Press titles at your local bookstore or order by calling 1-800-447-9778. You can also shop online at www.esri.com/esripress. Outside the United States, contact your local ESRI distributor.

ESRI Press titles are distributed to the trade by the following:

In North America:
Ingram Publisher Services
Toll-free telephone: (800) 648-3104
Toll-free fax: (800) 838-1149
E-mail: customerservice@ingrampublisherservices.com

In the United Kingdom, Europe, and the Middle East:
Transatlantic Publishers Group Ltd.
Telephone: 44 20 7373 2515
Fax: 44 20 7244 1018
E-mail: richard@tpgltd.co.uk

Cover design and production   Jennifer Campbell
Interior design and production   Jennifer Campbell and Jennifer Hasselbeck
Image editing   Jay Loteria
Editing   Michael Kataoka
Copyediting and proofreading   Tiffany Wilkerson
Permissions   Kathleen Morgan
Printing coordination   Cliff Crabbe and Lilia Arias

On the cover
Cover data from ESRI Data & Maps 2006, courtesy of ArcWorld Supplement, and National Geophysical Data Center.

To R. G. K. for listening to me talk about geospatial education for 15 years.

————K. K.

To Holly, Andrew, Zak, and Abby for their patience and support, always.

————B. K.

Contents

Preface

We have written this book to provide you with an opportunity to build your geographic information system (GIS) skills beyond the basics. The scenario-based activities in this book will both stretch your GIS knowledge and help build a bridge between your classroom experience and the centers of government, law enforcement, research, and other real-world entities that rely on GIS technology to make important decisions.

Our World GIS Education, Level 4: Making Spatial Decisions Using GIS puts actual spatial data into your hands—or more precisely, your computer—to analyze, interpret, and apply to various scenarios, including disasters and emergencies. You will make the type of decisions that affect a family, a community, or a nation.

The projects in this book involve GIS mapmaking, of course, but also will help you hone your critical thinking and decision-making skills. We have chosen scenarios we think are relevant, thought-provoking, and applicable to a broad range of studies, not just geography. We also think you'll have fun finding solutions to challenging problems.

This book comes with two DVDs. One contains the GIS data, worksheets, and other documents you will need to complete the projects. The other DVD contains a 180-day trial version of ArcView 9.2 software. This trial software requires the Microsoft Windows 2000 or Windows XP operating system. It is not supported on Windows Vista. This book also provides information about online resources.

Our World GIS Education is a four-book series of comprehensive GIS instruction for students of all ages, from elementary school level to college undergraduates. The series builds on the solid foundation of *Mapping Our World: GIS Lessons for Educators,* the popular ESRI Press book geared to middle- or high-school classrooms.

You need not have completed the other books in the series to benefit from *Making Spatial Decisions Using GIS,* but this is an advanced text that presumes you have some prior GIS knowledge. The technical prerequisites are outlined in the introduction, which also explains how to use the book, organize your workflow, and evaluate your work product. The introduction includes a summary of all five modules.

We have provided worksheets for your convenience. They will help you follow the exercises by logging answers to questions along the way and keeping track of the work to be completed. Your instructor has supplemental resources available to assist you with the projects in this book.

We have both spent much of our teaching careers connecting students to geospatial data. We hope you enjoy working on the activities in this book as much as we did in creating them. Work hard and have fun!

——— *Kathryn Keranen and Robert Kolvoord*

About the authors

Kathryn Keranen, a retired teacher, was instrumental in introducing GPS, GIS, and remote sensing into the geosystems curriculum in Fairfax County, Virginia. Since retiring, she has been a private consultant and an authorized K–12 ESRI instructor. She has consulted for various universities and is an adjunct instructor at James Madison University and Towson University.

Robert Kolvoord holds a PhD from Cornell University and is a professor of integrated science and technology at James Madison University. His main research interests are in the use of geospatial technologies in K–12 classrooms. At the University of Arizona, he was a founder of the nonprofit Center for Image Processing in Education. He has given workshops and presentations around the world in the use of data visualization technology in education.

Acknowledgments

We would like to thank all those who helped make this book possible.

At ESRI: Laura Bowden, who managed this project; David Davis, who fine-tuned the exercises; and Joseph Kerski, Charlie Fitzpatrick, Isaac Henson, Angela Lee, and Ann Johnson, each of whom provided valuable input. Nick Frunzi, ESRI Educational Services director; and Jack Dangermond, ESRI founder and president, deserve special thanks for their vision and support of this project.

At ESRI Press: Mike Kataoka, who edited the content; Jennifer Campbell, Savitri Brant, and Jennifer Hasselbeck, who designed the book; Michael Law, who refined the cartography; Kathleen Morgan, who oversaw permissions; Tiffany Wilkerson, who copyedited the manuscript; and Jay Loteria, who handled digital content. Judy Hawkins, former ESRI Press manager, and her successor, Peter Adams, provided outstanding leadership.

We are especially grateful to Tom Casady, chief of the Lincoln, Nebraska, Police Department; Tom Conry, GIS manager for Fairfax County, Virginia; and the Houston, Texas, Police Department's public affairs office for providing data and other essential material.

We also want to acknowledge the wonderful students and teachers with whom we get to work and who contributed time and talent to this project: Paul Rittenhouse and his Geospatial Semester students at Western Albemarle High School in Crozet, Virginia; Margaret Chernosky from Bangor High School in Bangor, Maine; Sallie Hill from the Orange County Schools, Orange County, Virginia; the fall 2007 GIS and the Environment class at James Madison University; and Tracy Campbell and Alicia Laroche, students in Geography and Integrated Science and Technology at James Madison University.

Introduction

Geographic information system (GIS) technology is a powerful way to analyze spatial data and is used in many industries to support decision making. From reassigning police personnel on the beat to locating a new housing development, GIS is at the center of important decisions. In *Our World GIS Education, Level 4: Making Spatial Decisions,* you will have a chance to analyze GIS data and learn to make and support spatial decisions.

This scenario-based book presents five modules, each with real-world situations designed to expand your GIS skills as you make decisions using actual GIS data. The projects involve the complicated, sometimes messy spatially related issues professionals from many disciplines face each day. The scenarios are not just step-by-step recipes for you to learn new GIS skills but opportunities to develop your critical-thinking prowess as well. As is true in so many situations, there's more than one "right answer," and you will have to decide the best solution for the problem at hand.

How to use this book

The scenario-based problems in this book presume that you have prior experience using GIS and are able to perform basic tasks using ArcGIS software (we're more specific about our expectations in the "Prior GIS experience" section).

Each of the five modules in this book follows the same format. Project 1 gives step-by-step instructions to explore a scenario. You answer questions and complete tables on a worksheet provided in the book and on your DVD. You reach decisions to resolve the central problem. Project 2 provides a slightly different scenario and the requisite data without step-by-step directions. You need to apply what you learned in project 1. Finally, each module includes an "On your own" section that suggests different scenarios you can explore by locating and downloading data and reproducing the analysis from the guided projects.

You can work through the modules in any order or as assigned by your instructor. You can also do just project 1 or both projects in each module.

GIS workflow

One major difference between these modules and other GIS-based lessons you may have done, including those in the three previous *Our World* books, is our focus on the GIS workflow: documenting and being systematic about the problem-solving process. Following a consistent GIS workflow is an important part of becoming a GIS professional.

We recommend the following GIS workflow:

1. Define the problem or scenario.
2. Identify the deliverables (mostly maps) needed to support the decision.
3. Identify, collect, organize, and examine the data needed to address the problem.
4. Document your work:
    a. Create a process summary.
    b. Document your map.
    c. Set the environments.
5. Prepare your data.
6. Create a basemap or locational map.
7. Perform the geospatial analysis.
8. Produce the deliverables, draw conclusions, and present the results.

A more detailed explanation of the workflow is in the "Workflow" section on page xxi.

Process summary

The process summary is particularly important because it serves as a record of the steps you took in the analysis. It also allows others to repeat the analysis and verify or validate your results. A process summary might look something like this for an analysis of agricultural land in Vermont. It will, of course, vary for each project:

1. Examine the metadata using ArcCatalog.

Map document 1

1. Prepare a basemap of Vermont.
2. Symbolize counties in graduated color using the POP2000 field.
3. Label lakes and major rivers.
4. Prepare a presentation layout.
5. Save the map document.

Map document 2

1. Name the data frame percentage as agricultural land.
2. Add the land-cover raster.
3. Symbolize land-cover raster with unique values by land-cover type.
4. Measure/calculate the area of all land in Vermont.
5. Select agricultural land cover using the raster calculator.
6. Measure/calculate the area of agricultural land.
7. Calculate the percentage of agricultural land.
8. Prepare a presentation layout.
9. Save the map document.

The modules

Each module focuses on a different use of GIS for local-level decision making, ranging from establishing evacuation routes during a hazardous material spill to understanding the changing demographic of America's urban areas to analyzing crime patterns in a city.

Module 1
Hazardous emergency decisions

Accidents, natural disasters, and terrorist acts all involve chaotic homeland security situations that require a coordinated response based on sound information. GIS, when applied to these emergencies, saves lives and property. This module puts you at the scene of two highway emergencies in which hazardous materials threaten a wide area. Your GIS analysis will aid first responders who must deal with evacuating and sheltering people, rerouting traffic, and providing for helicopter access. You will create buffers, analyze traffic patterns, and assess the suitability of school sites as emergency shelters.

Module 2
Demographic decisions

Nearly half the world's population lives in cities; of the 19 largest cities in 2000, only four are in industrialized nations. Thus, the study of urban demographics spans the globe. In fact, in the twentieth century, the number of city dwellers increased 14-fold worldwide. Demographic data allows you to study population growth trends, aging, housing, income, education, and other factors that play a part in increased urbanization. This module focuses on Chicago and Washington, D.C., two metropolitan areas with complex demographic issues. You will analyze diversity indexes, examine 3D images, create histograms, and calculate housing values in this module.

Module 3
Law enforcement decisions

A geospatial approach to crime fighting helps decision makers deploy limited police resources—personnel, equipment, facilities—for maximum benefit. In this module, we focus on law enforcement in Houston, Texas, and Lincoln, Nebraska, two cities that have successfully incorporated GIS technology into their crime analysis and planning processes. You have the opportunity to use actual data to size up the crime situation in each city and recommend specific action plans based on your GIS analysis. This module involves buffer zones, geocoding, and mapping density. The maps you produce will be the type of effective visual representations that, in the real world, assist decision makers and inform citizens.

Module 4
Hurricane damage decisions

In 2005, Hurricanes Katrina, Rita, and Wilma destroyed homes, businesses, infrastructure, and natural resources along the Gulf and Atlantic coasts. In the aftermath of the storms, federal, state, and local governments, service agencies, and the private sector responded by helping to rebuild the hurricane-ravaged areas and restore the local economies. GIS helped responders assess damage, monitor the weather, coordinate relief efforts, and track health hazards, among many other critical tasks, by providing relevant and readily available data, maps, and images. In this module, you will access some of the same data that guided critical decisions, such as funding and safety measures, in the wake of Hurricanes Katrina and Wilma. You will map elevations and bathymetry, analyze flooded areas and storm surges, and pinpoint vulnerable infrastructure. In the real world, this process saves lives, time, and money.

Module 5
Location decisions

There's an abundance of spatial data out there to help pinpoint the where. Where should I buy a house? Where should I establish my business? GIS can help gather, analyze, and visualize data to create reliable location intelligence that results in sound decisions. In this module, you will apply similar GIS processes for completely different purposes. Although the scenarios are fictitious, the locations and the data are real. You will study the rapidly growing area of Maricopa County, Arizona, to find a home for a doctor and a teacher with specific requirements. Then, in project two, the scene shifts to Ohio where the task at hand is to find the perfect spot for the fictitious Central Ohio College for the Arts' student radio station. In this module, you will examine census data, work with weighted overlays, and adjust map projections. These spatial skills can be applied to countless siting decisions large and small.

Assessing your work

Your instructor will talk with you about assessment, but you can assess your own work before handing it in. The items below will help ensure your presentation maps are the best they can be. Think about each of these items as you finish your maps and write up your work.

Map composition

Do your maps have the following elements?

- Title (addresses the major theme in your analysis)
- Legend
- Scale
- Compass rose
- Author (your name)

Classification

Did you make reasonable choices for the classifications of the different layers on your maps? Is the symbology appropriate for the various layers?

- For quantitative data, is there a logical progression from low to high values and are they clearly labeled?
- For qualitative data, did you make sure not to imply any ranking in your legend?

Scale and projection

- Is the map scale appropriate for your problem?
- Have you used an appropriate map projection?

Implied analysis

- Did you correctly interpret the color, pattern, and shape of your symbologies?
- Does any text you've written inform the reader of the map's intended use?

Design and aesthetics

- Are your maps visually balanced and attractive?
- Can you distinguish the various symbols for different layers in your maps?

Effectiveness of map

- How well do the map components communicate the story of your map?
- Do the map components take into account the interests and expertise of the intended audience?
- Are the map components of appropriate size?

By thinking about these items as you produce maps and do your analysis, you'll make your maps the most effective they can be at solving the problems in each module. See the "Cartographic information" section in the back of the book for more information on cartography basics.

Prior GIS experience

In these modules, we presume that you have used the ArcGIS software before and that you can do the following tasks:

- Navigate and find data on local drives, on network drives, and on CDs and DVDs
- Name files and save them in a known location
- Use ArcCatalog to connect to a folder
- Use ArcCatalog to preview a data layer and look at its metadata
- Add data to ArcMap by dragging layers from ArcCatalog or using the Add Data button
- Rearrange layers in the table of contents
- Identify the table of contents and the map window in ArcMap and know the purpose of each
- Use the following tools:
    - Identify
    - Zoom in
    - Zoom out
    - Full extent
    - Pan
    - Find
    - Measure
- Symbolize a layer by category or quantity
- Open the attribute table for a data layer
- Select features by attribute
- Label features
- Select features on a map and clear selection
- Work with tables
- Make a basic layout with map elements
- Use the drawing tools to place a graphic on the map

If you need some review, there are many great resources available, including *Our World Book 2: Mapping Our World Using GIS, Our World Book 3: Analyzing Our World Using GIS,* and *GIS Tutorial* from ESRI Press, and ArcGIS Desktop Help online.

ArcGIS Desktop software

The projects in this book use ArcGIS Desktop software. ArcGIS Desktop is part of the ESRI family of GIS software products. Each ArcGIS Desktop product includes two applications: ArcMap and ArcCatalog. ArcMap is used to display and edit geographic data, perform GIS analysis, and create professional-quality maps, graphs, and reports. ArcCatalog is designed for browsing, managing, and documenting geographic data.

The DVD also includes three ArcGIS Desktop extension products used in this book—ArcGIS 3D Analyst, ArcGIS Network Analyst, and ArcGIS Spatial Analyst. ArcGIS 3D Analyst includes the ArcScene and ArcGlobe applications, which are used for three-dimensional visualization and exploration of geographic data. ArcGIS Network Analyst and ArcGIS Spatial Analyst provide tools for specialized analysis tasks.

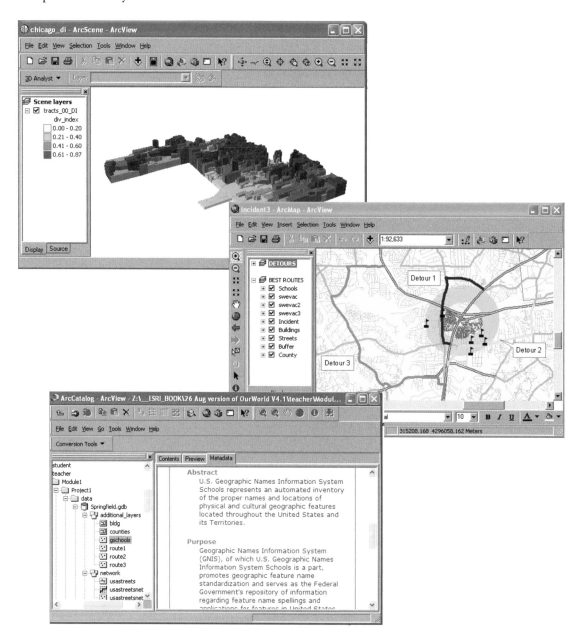

ArcGIS Desktop includes three license levels: ArcView, ArcEditor, and ArcInfo. ArcView, ArcEditor, and ArcInfo all look and work the same—they differ only in how much they can do. ArcEditor does more than ArcView, and ArcInfo does more than ArcEditor. The DVD included with this book includes the ArcView license of ArcGIS software, but all ArcGIS Desktop products can share the same maps and data.

Setting up the software and data

Using the DVDs

This book comes with two DVDs. One contains a 180-day trial edition of ArcView for Microsoft Windows. The other DVD contains the data, worksheets, and other documents required for the GIS projects. Refer to the installation guides at the back of the book for detailed system requirements and instructions on how to install the software data. The data license agreement is found at the back of the book and on the data DVD.

If you do not feel comfortable installing programs on your computer, please be sure to ask your campus technology specialist for assistance. The software and data on the DVDs needs to be installed on the hard drive of all computers you will use to complete these modules. Installations on a computer network server are not recommended nor supported.

Metadata

Metadata (information about the data) is included for all of the GIS data provided on the Data and Resources DVD. The metadata includes a description of the data, where it came from, a definition for each attribute field, and other useful information. This metadata can be viewed in ArcCatalog. In each project, one of the first things you will do is explore the metadata for the various layers.

Troubleshooting ArcGIS

Exercise instructions are written assuming the user interface and user preferences have the default settings. Unless you are working with a fresh installation of the software, however, chances are you will encounter some differences between the instructions and what you see on your screen. This is because ArcMap stores settings from a previous session. This could vary which toolbars are visible, where toolbars are located, the width of the table of contents, or whether or not the map scale changes when the window is resized.

A list of commonly encountered troubles and their solutions can be found on this book's Web site, www.esri.com/ourworldgiseducation. You may want to print out this list for reference. If you have other software questions relating to this book, you can send e-mail to learngis@esri.com with your questions.

The companion Web site

Besides solutions to common problems, the Web site places a variety of GIS resources and other helpful information at your fingertips. For example, you'll want to check the Web site's "Resources by Module" section for specific resources, Web links, or changes when you get ready to start a particular project. Any significant changes or corrections to the book will also be posted here.

Workflow

Addressing and analyzing a problem using GIS requires a structured approach similar to the problem-solving techniques you've done in other disciplines using other tools. With this approach you'll be certain to develop a solution that can be shared with and repeated by other GIS users, and you'll be able to communicate your results successfully to a broad audience.

In this book, use the following steps to define our GIS workflow or procedure. In each project, you'll address each step, in order, as you explore the problems and develop a solution or arrive at a decision. This is not the only way to work through a geospatial problem, but it is widely used in practice. Here are the steps explored in detail in the following pages:

1. Define the problem or scenario.
2. Identify the deliverables needed to support the decision.
3. Identify, collect, organize, and examine the data needed to address the problem.
4. Document your work.
5. Prepare your data.
6. Create a basemap or locational map.
7. Perform the geospatial analysis.
8. Produce the deliverables, draw conclusions, and present the results.

1. Define the problem or scenario

This is perhaps the most difficult part of the entire process. You must define what issue you are trying to address from a sometimes complicated sea of information and perhaps competing interests. This book presents real-world scenarios to help you with this process. You should always try to focus on the core issue in any situation calling for geospatial analysis. What decision needs to be made? Who is going to make it? What do people need to know to make a rational decision?

One approach is to write down a short description of the problem, including the general scenario, the stakeholders, and the specific issues that need to be addressed. It also helps to think about what decisions will ultimately be made using the data. Of course, the scenarios in this book require geospatial analysis using GIS software to solve problems. Other kinds of analyses may be included in these scenarios, but the focus will be on geospatial problem-solving.

2. Identify the deliverables needed to support the decision

After you've defined the problem, you need to think about what maps and other visualizations you'll produce to help you analyze and solve the problem. These may include the following:

- Maps
- Charts
- Tables of calculations
- Written analysis

By envisioning these maps, you'll be able to identify the data required for your analysis. You'll also be able to determine if you've defined your problem in sufficient detail to develop a solution. Along with specifying your data requirements, your list of deliverables will also guide your analysis. These first steps of your workflow are very iterative. You may need to go through them a few times before you're convinced that you're ready to begin your analysis. In many projects, they're also the most complicated steps.

3. Identify, collect, organize, and examine the data needed to address the problem

Once you've defined your problem and identified the deliverables, it is time to search for data. As a starting point, you should consider finding data for a basemap and data to solve the problem you've defined. In many instances, you'll have data at hand that will allow you to pursue your analysis. This data may have been provided for you (as in the first two projects of each module) or it may be part of a collection of data where you're working. It may come from the ESRI Data and Maps collection of DVDs. However, in some instances you may need to get data from other sources, such as Web sites, or you may need to collect your own data. If you need to do some sort of field study to collect your data, you'll want to be sure to develop a clear protocol for taking data and follow it consistently. You will also want to think carefully about the design of a database to hold your measurements.

In all cases, you should be careful to identify your data sources and make sure you have permission to use the data for your particular problem. You should make sure all data layers have appropriate metadata that describes various aspects of the data, including the creator of the data, its map projection, and the attributes included. You'll also want to know if you have vector or raster data layers and the accuracy or resolution of each layer.

As you collect the data for your analysis, it is strongly recommended that you adopt a standard for how you organize and store this data. This will make your analysis much easier, and you'll be able to quickly find different layers and share your work with others. A standard directory structure looks like this:

- Project folder
- Data folder containing all data layers
- Document folder containing all project documentation
- Project.mxd (this is the ArcGIS map document)

You must be able to both read and write to all folders within the project folder. You can place the project folder at a location that's convenient in the network structure in which you work. Each module shows you how to save your data with relative paths to make data sharing even easier.

When you obtain data from other sources, you'll often want to take a quick peek at the data to make sure you understand what it actually represents. Remember, these first steps of your workflow are very iterative. You may need to go through them a few times before you're convinced that you're ready to begin your analysis. In some instances, you may need to adjust your problem definition to let you use the available data, or the deliverables may need to be modified to make the analysis possible. In many projects, these first few steps are the most complicated.

4. Document your work

Documenting your project and creating a process summary is critical to keeping track of the various steps in your analysis. To document your project, go to the File menu and select Document

Properties. In the dialog box that appears, you can enter some of the basic information about your project. A process summary is simply a text document that keeps track of the different steps you use in your analysis. Too often, documentation of GIS work is left to the end of the project or is not done at all. You're encouraged to start your process summary early in each project and keep up with it as you proceed.

5. Prepare the data

Accurate GIS analysis may call for changing the units in which measurements will be made. You will also want to know the units in which various quantities are measured; are the elevations in feet or meters above sea level? You may need to provide geographic references to certain quantities, such as properly locating addresses or adding GPS-based data to your map display. You will be guided through these steps in the different projects.

6. Create a basemap or locational map

Finally, you're ready to make maps and perform your geospatial analysis. Your first step in this process should always be to build a locational or basemap that shows the area you are studying. A basemap will typically contain the major features of the area such as roads and streams, and it will help orient you geographically to the area and its features. This is a good practice when solving any geospatial problem as it will give you a sense of the scale of your study area and the different features that may dominate that area.

7. Perform the geospatial analysis

Now it is time to get down to the problem solving. In this step, you'll apply the different geospatial tools to the data you've compiled. These tools include selecting by attribute or location, classifying, interpolating, map algebra, measuring area, or a wide variety of other techniques. The point of your analysis is to produce the deliverables that you specified above and allow you to develop a solution to the problem you defined. Often you will find that the first set of analysis tools may not provide results that help solve the problem and you'll need to refine your analysis and try other tools or techniques. Even if you've been very careful and thorough in your planning to this point, geographic data never loses its ability to surprise you. As you work through the scenarios in this book, you will learn a variety of advanced analysis techniques.

8. Produce the deliverables, draw conclusions, and present the results

Finally, you're satisfied with your analysis and you're ready to complete your work. You will first need to complete your deliverables (as defined earlier in the process). This may mean making map layouts, graphs, charts, or tables. You'll also want to finish documenting your analysis process. Remember to keep the principles of good cartographic design in mind when you make your deliverables. The ESRI "Introduction to Map Design" is an excellent primer on creating high-quality maps. It is included in the documents folder as intrcart.pdf.

You will also need to write a report that states your conclusions and justifies them, using the deliverables you have produced. Always keep the audience in mind as you're preparing to report your results. A technically savvy audience will have very different needs from a group of high-level decision makers. Remember to finish your process summary.

Congratulations! You've finished your project and used a GIS workflow that will lead to success.

MODULE 1

Hazardous emergency decisions

Introduction

Accidents, natural disasters, and terrorist acts all involve chaotic homeland security situations that require a coordinated response based on sound information. GIS, when applied to these emergencies, saves lives and property. This module puts you at the scene of two highway emergencies in which hazardous materials threaten a wide area. Your GIS analysis will aid first responders who must deal with evacuating and sheltering people, rerouting traffic, and providing for helicopter access. You will create buffers, analyze traffic patterns, and assess the suitability of school sites as emergency shelters. You will use the ArcGIS Network Analyst extension in this module.

Projects in this module:

- **An explosive situation in Springfield, Virginia**

- **Skirting the spill in Mecklenburg County, North Carolina**

- **On your own**

Module worksheets

The student worksheet files can be found on the Data and Resources DVD.

Project 1 student sheet

- File name: Springfield_student_worksheet.doc
- Location: OurWorld4\Module1\Project1\documents
- Document length: 4 pages
- Worksheet for "An explosive situation in Springfield, Virginia." A form for answering questions, completing tables, and tracking work to be handed in.

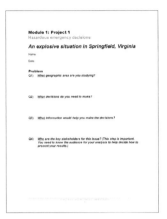

Project 2 student sheet

- File name: Mecklenburg_student_worksheet.doc
- Location: OurWorld4\Module1\Project2\documents
- Document length: 3 pages
- Worksheet for "Skirting the spill in Mecklenburg County, North Carolina." A form for answering questions, completing tables, and tracking work to be handed in.

Module 1: Project 1 ●

An explosive situation in Springfield, Virginia

Scenario

Shortly before 4:00 AM on June 2, 1999, a tractor-trailer rig carrying 34,000 pounds of highly explosive black powder overturned at the "mixing bowl"—the heavily-traveled convergence of Interstates 95 and 495—in Springfield, Virginia. The flatbed tractor-trailer slid from the off-ramp from northbound I-95 onto westbound I-495. The Virginia State Police and the Fairfax County Police jointly provided personnel to coordinate the accident response.

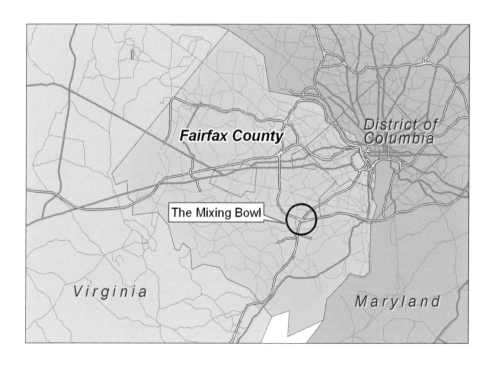

Problem

Fairfax County police officers arrived first, immediately pinpointing the location with GPS receivers and identifying the hazardous substance. The officers accessed the Material Safety Data Sheet (MSDS) online for information about evacuation zones. An MSDS is required by the federal government and provides emergency personnel with proper procedures for handling or working with a particular hazardous substance. Officers needed maps showing the vulnerable area surrounding the accident, an estimate of the number of households to evacuate, suggestions for possible shelters for the evacuees, and a traffic analysis designating detours for vehicles. The analysis would include suggestions for a helicopter landing site both for medical evacuation and to transport personnel for logistical support. The helicopter landing site needed to be near the incident and evacuation zone.

In applying GIS to a problem, you must have a very clear understanding of the problem or scenario. We find it helpful to answer these four questions, which test your understanding and divide the problem into smaller problems that are easier to solve.

Q1 *What geographic area are you studying? (Record answers on your worksheet.)*

Q2 *What decisions do you need to make?*

Q3 *What information would help you make the decisions?*

Q4 *Who are the key stakeholders for this issue? (This step is important. You need to know the audience for your analysis to help decide how to present your results.)*

Deliverables

After identifying the problem you're trying to solve, you need to envision the kinds of data displays (maps, graphs, and tables) that will address the problem. We recommend the following deliverables for this exercise:

1. A map of Fairfax County showing roads and schools.
2. A map of buffered areas around the incident. The map should show the following:
   a. Shelter locations
   b. Residences to be evacuated
   c. Helicopter landing site
3. A map showing redirected traffic patterns both around the incident and within the buffer zone.

M ● ○ ○ ○ ○
P ● ○ ○

Examine the data

The next step in your workflow is to identify, collect, and examine the data for the Springfield accident analysis. Here, we've identified and collected the data layers you will need. Explore the data to better understand both the raster and vector feature classes in this exercise.

You will use ArcCatalog to preview the GIS data and explore the metadata associated with each feature class. Thoroughly investigate the data layers to understand how they'll help you address the problem. The spatial coordinate system, the resolution of the data, and the attribute data are all important pieces of information about a feature class.

1. Open ArcCatalog and connect to the folder **OurWorld4\Module1\Project1\ data.**

2. Expand the data folder in the Catalog tree and double-click the Springfield geodatabase. The geodatabase holds two feature classes and an image.

3. Click the Preview tab, then preview the geography and table for each item in the data folder.

Q5 *Using ArcCatalog, investigate the metadata and complete this table on your worksheet:*

Layer	Publication Information: Who Created The Data?	Time Period Data Is Relevant	Spatial Horizontal Coordinate System	Data Type	Resolution For Rasters	Attribute Values
bldg	Fairfax County, VA	2007			N/A	Building attributes
aerial						N/A
counties					N/A	
gschools					N/A	N/A

4. Close ArcCatalog.

Now that you've explored the available data, you're almost ready to begin your analysis. First you need to start a process summary, document your project, and set the project environments.

Organize and document your work

Step 1: Examine the directory structure

The next phase in a GIS project is to carefully keep track of the data and your calculations. You will work with a number of different files and it is important to keep them organized so you can easily find them. The best way to do this is to have a folder for your project that contains a data folder. For this project, the folder called **OurWorld4\Module1\Project1** will be your project folder. Make sure that it is stored in a place where you have write access. You can store your data inside the results folder. The results folder already contains an empty geodatabase named **project1_results.** Save your map documents inside the **OurWorld4\Module1\Project1\results** folder.

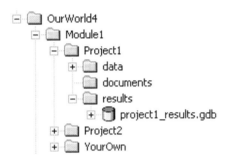

Step 2: Create a process summary

The process summary is just a list of the steps you used to do your analysis. We suggest using a simple text document for your process summary. Keep adding to it as you do your work to avoid forgetting any steps. The list below shows an example of the first few entries in a process summary:

1. Explore the data.
2. Produce a map of Fairfax County showing roads and schools.
3. Identify the incident.
4. Prepare a buffer zone around the incident.

Step 3: Document the map

You need to add descriptive properties to every map document you produce. Use the same descriptive properties listed below for every map document in the module or individualize the documentation from map to map.

1. Open ArcMap and save the map document as **incident1.** (Save it in the **OurWorld4\Module1\Project1\results** folder.)

2. From the File menu, choose Document Properties and in the dialog box add a title, author, and some descriptive text.

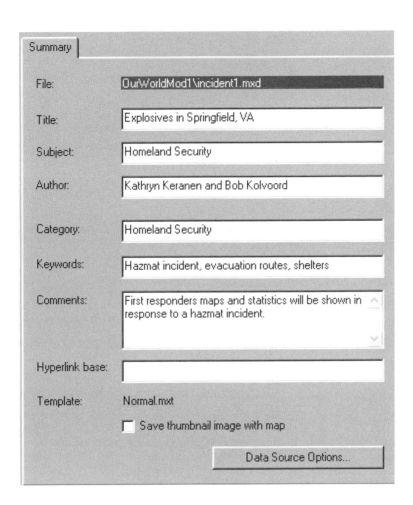

3. Click Data Source Options and then click the radio button to store relative paths of data sources. Click OK in both dialog boxes.

Storing relative paths for data sources allows ArcMap to automatically find all relevant data if you move your project folder to a new location or computer.

Step 4: Set the environments

In GIS analysis, you will often get data from several sources and this data may be in different coordinate systems and/or map projections. When using GIS to perform area calculations, you would like your result to be in familiar units, such as miles or kilometers. Data in an unprojected geographic coordinate system has units of decimal degrees, which are difficult to interpret. Thus, your calculations will be more meaningful if all the feature classes involved are in the same map projection. Fortunately, ArcMap can do much of this work for you if you set certain environment variables and data frame properties. In this section, you'll learn how to change these settings.

To display your data correctly, you'll need to set the coordinate system for the data frame. When you add data with a defined coordinate system, ArcMap will automatically set the data frame's projection to match the data. If you add subsequent layers that have a coordinate system different from the data frame, they are automatically projected on-the-fly to the data frame's coordinate system.

1. From the View menu, choose Data Frame Properties. Click the Coordinate System tab. Select Predefined, Projected Coordinate Systems, UTM, NAD 1983, Zone 18N, and click OK.

Before using ArcToolbox tools to make your calculations, you will establish some general environment settings that apply to all of the tools you'll be using. The analysis environment includes the workspace where results will be placed, and the extent, cell size, and coordinate system for the results.

2. Open ArcToolbox, right-click any empty space within ArcToolbox and choose Environments.

3. Expand General Settings.

By default, inputs and outputs are placed in your current workspace, but you can redirect the output to another workspace such as your results folder.

4. Set the Current Workspace as **OurWorld4\Module1\Project1\data\ Springfield.gdb.**

5. Set the Scratch Workspace as **OurWorld4\Module1\Project1\results\ project1_results.gdb.**

6. For Output Coordinate System, select "Same as Display."

7. Click OK.

M ● ○ ○ ○ ○
P ● ○ ○

Analysis

Once you've examined the data, completed map documentation, and set the environments, you are ready to begin the analysis and to complete the displays you need to address the problem. A good place to start any GIS analysis is to produce a basemap to better understand the distribution of features in the geographic area you're studying. First, you will prepare a basemap of Springfield, Virginia, showing streets and schools.

Step 1: Create a basemap of Fairfax County

1. From the Springfield geodatabase\Additional Layers, add counties and gschools.

2. From the Springfield geodatabase\Network Layers, add usastreets. The Geographic Coordinate System Warning Menu appears. Click Transformations and choose GCS_WGS_1984 and click OK and then click Close.

3. Symbolize the schools appropriately and import the usa_street layer file. In the Import Symbology Matching dialog box that appears, click OK.

4. Label Interstate 95 and Interstate 495. Interstate 495 is the Capital Beltway and it encircles Washington, D.C. Interstate 95 is the main north-to-south highway along the east coast. Both roads are heavily traveled.

5. Save the map document.

▶ Deliverable 1: A map of Fairfax County showing roads and schools.

Step 2: Identify incident and isolate areas of concern

Upon arriving at the scene, police recorded the coordinates of the incident location as 77°10'33.031"W and 38°47'20.626"N. After questioning the driver of the big rig, officers learned that the black powder was not heavily encased. Knowing the exact nature of the material allowed officers to use their MSDS database.

Open the MSDS stored in the documents folder and determine the extent of the evacuation area around the incident. The police designated an evacuation zone of 0.5 miles around the ramp where the incident occurred.

Q6 *How much area needs to be evacuated?*

The police team also designated shelters for evacuees within a half mile of the evacuated area.

A. Create buffers around the incident

1. Open a new map document and save as **incident2.**

11

2. Refer back to "Organize and document your work" and do the following:

   a. *Document the map.*

   b. *Set the data frame properties. They must be set for each data frame.*

   c. *Set the environments.*

3. Add the bldg, counties, and gschools from the Springfield geodatabase\ Additional Layers.

4. Add usastreets from the Springfield geodatabase/Network Layers. When the Warning appears, choose GCS_WGS_1984.

5. Use the Go to XY button on the Tools toolbar and locate the point where the incident occurred. (77°10'33.031"W and 38°47'20.626"N in DMS or 77.175842 and 38.789063 in Decimal Degrees.) Click the Add Point button.

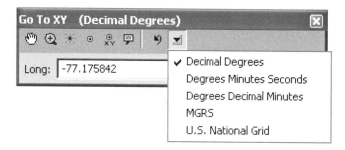

6. Zoom to the point.

7. Use the Select Feature tool and select the ramp where the incident occurred. Right-click usastreets and select Data. Select Export Data and export the selection to the project1_results.gdb in the results folder. Name the file **incident.** (Note: The file must be saved as a File and Personal Geodatabase feature class.)

8. Deselect the ramp and symbolize the incident layer so it can be easily seen.

9. Open ArcToobox and expand Analysis Tools, expand Proximity, and double-click Multiple Ring Buffer.

   a. *Set the Input feature as incident.*

   b. *Set the Output feature as buffer (and save it in the results folder).*

   c. *Distances are* **0.5** *and* **1.** *(Type the number in the Distances box and then click the + button.)*

   d. *Make sure the Buffer Unit is Miles.*

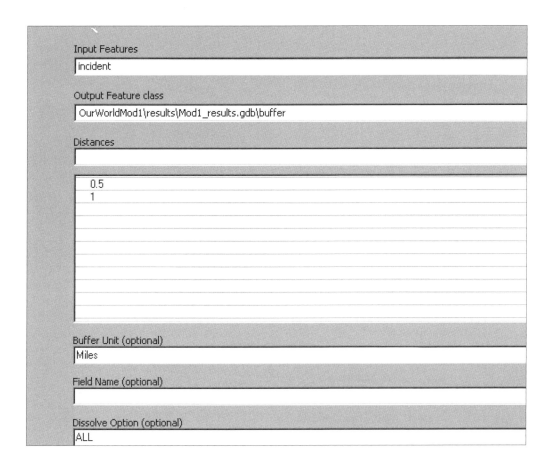

Input Features

| incident |

Output Feature class

| OurWorldMod1\results\Mod1_results.gdb\buffer |

Distances

| |

| 0.5 |
| 1 |

Buffer Unit (optional)

| Miles |

Field Name (optional)

| |

Dissolve Option (optional)

| ALL |

10. Click OK.

11. Zoom the map view so you can see the entire buffer.

12. Display the buffer by unique value with distance as the value field.

13

13. Save the map document.

B. Locate evacuation areas and shelters

You need to isolate schools that are within one-half to one mile from the accident scene. These schools are potential shelters for evacuees. Note that there are no schools within one-half mile of the incident, therefore no schools need to be evacuated.

1. In ArcToolbox, expand Analysis Tools, expand Extract, and double-click Clip.

    a. The input feature is gschools.

    b. Clip Features should be set to buffer.

    c. Store the output feature in your results geodatabase and name it **schools.**

    d. Click Save and OK.

2. Remove gschools and symbolize the isolated schools.

To decide how many people must be evacuated, you must isolate the residences within the 0.5-mile evacuation area.

M ● ○ ○ ○ ○
P ● ○ ○

3. Select the buildings from bldg that are single family residential. (Hint: query for Type = SFR. C stands for commercial, I for Industrial, P for Public, and SFR stands for Single Family Residential.)

4. Select the 0.5-mile buffer area only and use the selected buffer. (Hint: Hold down the shift key and use the Select Features tool from the Toolbar to select the 0.5-mile buffer and maintain the building selection.)

5. Clip the bdlg layer and name the file **sfr** and store it in the results folder.

6. Remove bldg and deselect the 0.5-mile buffer zone.

Q7 *How many single-family residences are in the danger area?*

Q8 *Where are the residential buildings located?*

Q9 *What school would work best as a designated shelter for the people evacuated in the southeast quadrant? (Hint: High schools are usually better equipped to handle large numbers of people.)*

Q10 *What school would work best as a designated shelter for the people evacuated in the southwest quadrant? (Hint: The school located nearest to the incident would be the best.)*

7. Name the data frame **buildings and shelters.**

8. Save the map document.

C. Choose helicopter landing site

1. Right-click the buildings and shelters data frame and select copy. Go to the Edit menu and select paste.

2. Change the name of the pasted data frame to **helicopter site.**

3. Add the raster dataset aerial.

4. Make the 0.5-mile buffer hollow or turn on the Effects toolbar and swipe the buffer.

5. Examine the image closely by zooming in and out and pick a place that would be an appropriate helicopter landing site. It should be close to the incident for medical and other evacuations and for the logistical transport of emergency personnel.

6. Place a graphic where you think an appropriate landing site would be and symbolize it appropriately.

7. Save your map document.

▷ **Deliverable 2: A map of buffered areas around the incident. The map should show the following:**

a. Shelter locations labeled

b. Residences that need to be evacuated

c. Helicopter landing site

For the next part of the exercise you will need to turn on the Network Analyst extension and display the Network Analyst toolbar.

1. Go to the Tools Menu and select Extensions.

2. Check Network Analyst and click Close.

3. To turn on the Network Analyst toolbar, go to the View menu and select Toolbars.

4. Select the Network Analyst toolbar and it will appear.

Step 3: Map detours and best routes to shelters

After the immediate area is secure and the houses to be evacuated have been identified, the redirection of traffic is critical. In this part of the exercise you will determine alternative traffic routes and identify intersections requiring a police presence.

A. Map detours around the accident scene

1. Open a new blank map document and save it as **incident3**.

2. Refer back to "Organize and document your work" and do the following:

    a. *Document the map.*

    b. *Set the data frame properties. They must be set for each data frame.*

    c. *Set the environments.*

3. Add the usastreetsnet from the Network Layers feature class. When asked if you want to add all feature classes, click No. The Geographic Coordinate System Warning Menu appears. Click Transformations and choose GCS_WGS_1984 and click OK, then click Close.

4. Add usastreets and in the Symbology tab in the Layers Properties dialog box, import the usastreets layer file.

5. Add counties from the Additional Layers feature class.

6. Add buffer, incident, schools, and sfr from the results folder. The Geographic Coordinate System Warning Menu appears. Click Transformations and choose GCS_WGS_1984, click OK and then click Close.

7. Zoom to the buffer layer.

8. Click the Network Analyst window button on the Network Analyst toolbar to open the dockable window.

9. In the Network Analyst toolbar, click the Network Analyst drop-down menu and click New Route. The Network Window now contains empty lists of Stops, Routes, and Barriers.

10. Right-click Stops (0) in the Network Analyst window and go to Load Locations. Load route1 from the Additional Layers feature class and click OK. When you load route1, stop 1 and 2 appear. These two stops are where road blocks will occur to block the highway. Using these stops, the software will calculate a path (route) around the closed road.

Q11 *What road(s) is (are) being closed by these two stops?*

Every street that carries traffic within the 0.5-mile buffer zone needs to be closed. First, you must identify the streets that cross into the buffer zone and then insert barriers to keep the traffic out.

11. Select the 0.5-mile buffer zone.

12. Select by location features from the usastreets that "are crossed by the outline of" buffer. Click OK. This selects all the streets that feed into the 0.5-mile buffer zone. This allows you to see which streets need to be closed.

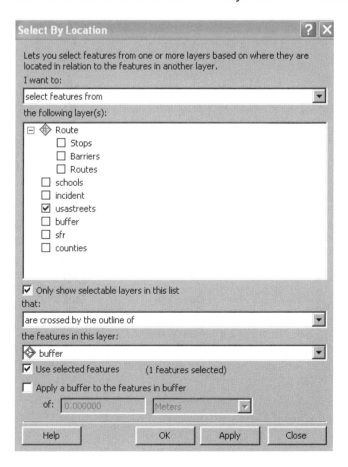

13. Add barriers.

a. *Click Barriers.*

 b. *Click the Create Network Location tool and place a barrier on every road that enters the 0.5-mile buffer zone.*

It is important that the barriers are actually placed on the roads. For accuracy, use the Magnifier. In the Window menu, click Magnifier to bring up the Magnifier window. You can drag the Magnifier window around by its title bar.

M ● ○ ○ ○ ○
P ● ○ ○

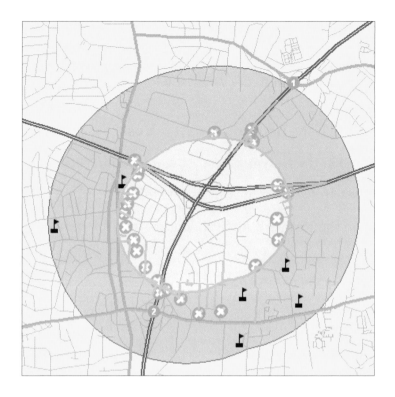

 14. After the barriers have been determined, click the Solve button in the Network Analyst toolbar.

A new alternative route is computed, avoiding the barriers.

15. Close the Magnifier window.

16. Right-click Routes (1) in the Network Analyst window and click Export Data.

17. Name the file **route1** and store it in your project1_results geodatabase.

18. Right-click Routes in the Network Analyst window and select Directions Window.

Q12 *What is the total distance of the Route 1 detour?*

You need to create two more alternative routes.

19. Right-click Barriers and select Export Data to save the barriers in your results folder so you don't have to add them again.

20. Name them **barriers.**

21. Deselect the intersected streets.

22. In the Network Analyst toolbar, click the Network Analyst drop-down menu and click New Route.

23. Right-click Stops (0) in the Network Analyst window and go to Load Locations. Load route2 from the Additional Layers feature class.

19

(Q13) *What road is being closed by these two stops?*

24. Right-click Barriers (0) in the Network Analyst window and go to Load Locations and load Barriers from the results folder.

25. Click the Solve button in the Network Analyst toolbar.

26. Right-click Routes (2) in the Network Analyst window and click Export Data.

27. Name the file **route2** and store it in your results folder.

28. Right-click Routes in the Network Analyst window and open the Directions window.

(Q14) *What is the total distance of the Route 2 detour?*

29. Repeat the above procedure for Route 3.

(Q15) *What road is being closed by these two stops?*

(Q16) *What is the total distance of the Route 3 detour?*

30. Name the data frame **detours.**

31. Save the map document.

B. Determine best routes to shelters

1. Copy the detours data frame.

2. Paste it and name the pasted data frame **best routes.**

3. Collapse the detours data frame.

4. Remove Route1, Route2, and Route3.

5. Zoom to the southern quadrant of the buffer zone. This is the location of residential buildings that have to be evacuated. The southeast quadrant evacuation center is Robert E. Lee High School. The southwest quadrant evacuation center is Lynbrook Elementary School. The police want to establish the best route for evacuees so officers can direct traffic.

6. In the southwest quadrant, the police are starting the evacuation route at 6780 Cabin John Rd., Springfield, VA, 22150, and ending at Lynbrook Elementary School. Prepare the best route so police can direct traffic. Record the mileage and the time.

7. In the Network Analyst toolbar, click the Network Analyst drop-down menu and click New Route.

8. Right-click Stops (0) and select Find Address.

9. Select springfield from the data folder as the address locator.

10. Enter **6780 Cabin John Rd** as the Street and click Find.

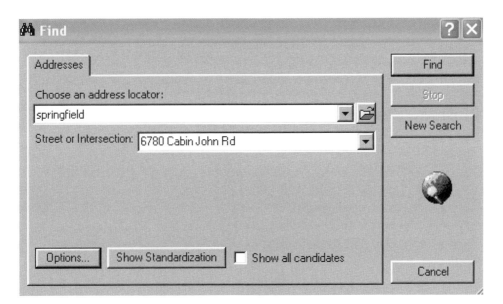

11. Right-click the address row to show the context menu and select Add Point. This puts a point at the 6780 Cabin John Rd. address.

12. Close the Find Menu.

13. In the Network Analyst toolbar, click the create Network Location tool and click the graphic point for the 6780 Cabin John Rd. address and then click Lynbrook Elementary School.

14. Click the Solve button in the Network Analyst toolbar to run the process and compute the best route.

15. To save the Route, right-click route(1) in the Network Analyst window and click Export Data. Save the route as **swevac** in the project1_results geodatabase.

16. Remove the route and symbolize swevac.

There are two designated evacuation routes for the southeast evacuation area:

1. The first route goes from 6015 Trailside Drive, Springfield, VA, 22150 to Robert E. Lee High School.
2. The second route starts at 6756 Bison St, goes to 6899 Bowie Drive and ends at Robert E. Lee High School.

21

17. Repeat steps 11–15 for these two designated routes and name the files **seevac2** and **seevac3.** Remove the routes.

18. Save the map document.

▶ **Deliverable 3: A map showing redirected traffic patterns both around the incident and within the buffer zone.**

Once your analysis is complete, you're not done. You still need to develop a solution to the original problem and present your results in a compelling way to the police in this particular situation. The presentation of your various data displays must explain what they show and how they contribute to solving the problem.

Presentation

Write a report documenting your analysis and addressing how you identified the evacuation shelters, road intersections to be closed, and the detour routes. You must explain the spatial patterns you see and describe the implications of your calculations and analysis for this problem. Remember that your audience probably lacks your in-depth knowledge of GIS, so you'll need to communicate your results in a way that they'll be able to understand and use.

M ● ○ ○ ○ ○
P ● ○ ○

Skirting the spill in Mecklenburg County, North Carolina

Scenario

Hazardous materials spills are a source of great concern for local and state law enforcement. In this hypothetical scenario, a tanker truck carrying chlorine gas was westbound on Interstate 85 north of Charlotte in Mecklenburg County, North Carolina. The driver lost control of his truck between the two segments of Interstate 77. The truck left the road and overturned. The impact caused several cracks in the tanker and gas began slowly leaking. The weather was cloudy with no wind.

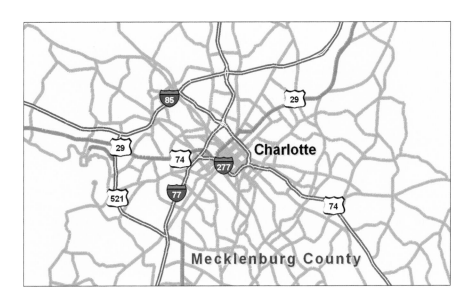

Problem

North Carolina state troopers arrived at the accident scene first, pinpointed the location with GPS receivers, and identified the leaking gas as chlorine. They then accessed the Material Safety Data Sheet (MSDS) for information about evacuation zones. (The MSDS sheet for chlorine is provided in the Documents folder.) The state troopers immediately needed maps showing the required evacuation zone around the incident, a rough estimate of the population to evacuate, and possible shelter sites for evacuees. They also needed a traffic analysis to determine how best to reroute vehicles and where to pick up evacuees. The response team sought suggestions for a helicopter landing site, both for medical evacuation and to transport personnel for logistical support. The helicopter landing site needed to be close to the incident and the areas of evacuation.

Reminder

It helps to divide a large problem such as this into a set of smaller tasks such as the following:

1. Identify the geographic study area.
2. Determine the sequence of steps in your study.
3. Identify the decisions to be made.
4. Develop the information required to make decisions.
5. Identify stakeholders for this issue.

Deliverables

We recommend the following deliverables for this problem:

1. A map of Mecklenburg County showing roads and schools.
2. A map of buffered areas around the incident. The map should show the following:
   a. Shelter locations
   b. An approximate number of households to be evacuated
   c. Helicopter landing site
3. A map showing redirected traffic patterns both around the incident and from within the buffer zone.

Examine the data

The data for this project is stored in the **OurWorld4\Module1\Project2\data** folder.

Reminder

You can explore the metadata in ArcCatalog. The table on the following page helps you organize this information.

Q1 *Investigate the metadata and complete this table on your worksheet:*

Layer	Publication Information: Who Created The Data?	Time Period Data Is Relevant	Spatial Horizontal Coordinate System	Data Type	Resolution For Rasters	Attribute Values
bklgrp	Tele Atlas North America, Inc., ESRI	2006			N/A	Demographic Attributes
aerial						N/A
gschools					N/A	N/A
usa-streets					N/A	

Organize and document your work

Reminder

1. Set up the proper directory structure.
2. Create a process summary.
3. Document the map.
4. Set the environments:
    a. Set the Data Frame Coordinate System to be the same as the aerial raster dataset.
    b. Set the Working Directory.
    c. Set the Scratch Directory.
    d. Set the Output Coordinate System to "Same as Display."

Analysis

An important first step in GIS analysis is to develop a basemap of your study area.

Complete deliverable 1 and answer the questions below to orient yourself to the study area.

▶ **Deliverable 1: A map of Mecklenburg County showing roads and schools.**

Q2 *What main road goes north to south?*

Q3 *What main road goes west to east?*

To continue your analysis you need to know the facts upon which the state troopers and first responders based their decision. The facts and timeline are as follows:

- The first North Carolina trooper on the scene reported the incident position as 80°50'38.76" W, 35°16'23.24"N (-80.8441, 35.273122).
- After talking to the trucker, troopers identified the leaking gas as chlorine.
- They contacted AccuWeather for a weather report. The weather for the rest of the day was cloudy with no wind.
- They carefully read the MSDS and decided to evacuate two miles around the incident and designate shelters that were within one-half mile of the outer perimeter of the evacuation zone.

Using all the information above, continue the analysis to prepare deliverable 2.

Reminder

When you create the multiple buffers, the distances should be 2 and 2.5 miles.

There is no building information with this exercise. You have to use the census block group data to estimate the number of households to evacuate within the two-mile zone.

Clip the block group and then calculate statistics using the households field to estimate the number of households to evacuate. It helps to show the block groups to be evacuated in graduated color by the number of households.

Q4 *Which quadrant has the most households to evacuate?*

Q5 *How many total households must be evacuated?*

Extending the project

Your instructor may choose for you to complete this optional exercise.

Create reports on your layout with the names of the schools to be evacuated and the schools that can be used for shelters. Go to Tools and Select Reports and then Create Reports.

Reminder

Because you have set the environments, you must copy and paste the existing Data Frame and rename the pasted data frame for the helicopter landing sites analysis.

▶ **Deliverable 2: A map of buffered areas around the incident. The map should show the following:**

a. **Shelter locations**
b. **An approximate number of households to be evacuated**
c. **Helicopter landing site**

The final deliverable consists of rerouting traffic both around the incident and from within the evacuation zone to shelters.

▶ **Deliverable 3: A map showing redirected traffic patterns both around the incident and from within the buffer zone.**

Refer to your process summary from module 1, project 1 and review the procedure for creating barriers and saving them. Create detours 1-5 using the given detour stops layers (detour1stops, detour2stops, etc.).

Q6 *Complete the following table on your worksheet:*

Detours	Mileage
1	
2	
3	
4	
5	

Based on a data analysis, the following schools were designated as shelters. Several were not in the designated half-mile area around the two-mile buffer zone. There were designated pickup areas where buses were sent to evacuate the people with no other means of transportation. The pickup areas and associated shelter schools are listed below:

Pick-up area	Designated school shelter
3201 Graham St.	Highland Mill Elementary School
2201 Lasalle St.	Johnson C. Smith University
3601 Beatties Ford Rd.	Oakdale Elementary
4451 Statesville Rd.	Winding Springs Elementary

Create routes from the pickup areas to each of the shelters. Hint—use the usa_streets address locator in the data folder.

Name them **route1, route2, route3,** and **route4,** respectively.

Presentation

Remember to keep in mind the interests and expertise of your audience as you prepare your presentation. Develop a solution to the original problem and present your results in a compelling way.

Module 1: Project 3 ● ● ● ○

On your own

You've worked through a guided activity on the impact of a hazardous materials spill and repeated that analysis in another community. In this section, you will reinforce the skills you've developed by researching and analyzing a similar scenario entirely on your own. First, you must identify your study area and acquire data for your analysis. There are many variations of this activity but consider choosing a scenario that has local impact. Think about chemicals that are transported through your community on railroads, pipelines, and highways. Identify locations such as nuclear power stations, oil refineries, fertilizer plants, gas stations, and dry cleaners that could be the source of hazardous spills. Don't forget the water. Rivers and lakes could be contaminated depending on where a spill occurs. There are many Web sites that contain extensive collections of Material Safety Data Sheets (MSDS). Make sure to access the appropriate MSDS for your hazardous material.

Refer to your process summary and the preceding module projects if you need help. Here are some basic steps to help you organize your work:

Research

Research the problem and answer the following questions:

1. What is the area of study?
2. What is the hazardous material and what are the MSDS constraints?

Obtain the data

Do you have access to baseline data? The ESRI Data and Maps Media Kit provides many of the layers of data that are needed for project work. Be sure to pay particular attention to the source of data and get the latest version. Older versions of the ESRI Data and Maps Media Kit are very useful for temporal comparison, so be sure to check the date.

For this exercise, it is imperative that you have access to ESRI Streetmap Data so you can use Network Analyst to calculate detours and evacuation routes. If you obtain data from your local GIS department, make sure to ask for a transportation network along with any other needed data.

If you do not have access to the ESRI Data and Maps Media Kit, you can obtain data from the following sources:

- http://www.esri.com/tiger
- http://www.geographynetwork.com
- http://www.nationalatlas.gov
- http://seamless.usgs.gov (This site allows you to download a high-resolution image.)

Workflow

After researching the problem and obtaining the data, you should do the following:

1. Write a brief scenario.
2. State the problem.
3. Define the deliverables.
4. Examine the data using ArcCatalog.
5. Set the directory structure, start your process summary, and document the map.
6. Decide what you need for the data frame coordinate system and the environments.
   a. What is the best projection for your work?
   b. Do you need to set a cell size or mask?
7. Start your analysis.
8. Prepare your presentation and deliverables.

Always remember to document your work in a process summary.

MODULE 2

Demographic decisions

Introduction

Nearly half the world's population currently lives in cities; of the 19 largest cities in 2000, only four are in industrialized nations. Thus, the study of urban demographics now spans the globe. In fact, in the twentieth century, the number of city dwellers increased 14-fold worldwide. Demographic data allows you to study population growth trends, aging, housing, income, education, and other factors that play a part in increased urbanization. This module focuses on Chicago and Washington, D.C., two metropolitan areas with complex demographic issues. You will analyze diversity indexes, examine 3D images, create histograms, and calculate housing values in this module.

Projects in this module:

- **For richer or poorer in Chicago**

- **Determining diversity in Washington, D.C.**

- **On your own**

Module worksheets

The student worksheet files can be found on the Data and Resources DVD.

Project 1 student sheet

- File name: Chicago_student_worksheet.doc
- Location: OurWorld4\Module2\Project1\documents
- Document length: 7 pages
- Worksheet for "For richer or poorer in Chicago." A form for answering questions, completing tables, and tracking work to be handed in.

Project 2 student sheet

- File name: Washington_student_worksheet.doc
- Location: OurWorld4\Module2\Project2\documents
- Document length: 3 pages
- Worksheet for "Determining diversity in Washington, D.C." A form for answering questions, completing tables, and tracking work to be handed in.

Module 2: Project 1

For richer or poorer in Chicago

Scenario

Chicago is the third largest city in the United States. Nearly 10 million people, representing a diverse ethnic and economic mix, live in its greater metropolitan area. In this exercise, Cook County, Illinois, which includes the urbanized area of Chicago, will serve as the focus for a study of demographic trends. The map below shows you the study area.

Problem

A local university's social science division needs maps and charts to explore the changing urban demographics of the Chicago metropolitan area and its relationship to Cook County over the past 10 years. A demographic research team is examining neighborhood integration and transition by measuring increasingly multiethnic and multiracial populations. The team would like to see maps of African-American, Caucasian, and Hispanic populations between 1990 and 2000. The team also would like to see diversity indexes of Cook County calculated and displayed for both 1990 and 2000. African-Americans, Caucasians, and Hispanics represent the largest ethnic/racial groups in Chicago. Finally the team wants to examine the impact of economics on diversity by studying the spatial distribution of median house value in 2000 and how that measure correlates to changing neighborhood settlement patterns. The researchers have requested that the data be displayed in 3D to engage their users. You must supply the researchers with a GIS analysis using the data and tools introduced below.

In applying GIS to a problem, you must have a very clear understanding of the problem or scenario. We find it helpful to answer these four questions, which test your understanding and divide the problem into a set of smaller problems that are easier to solve.

Q1 *What geographic area are you studying? (Record answers on your worksheet.)*

Q2 *What is the decision you need to make?*

Q3 *What information would help you make the decision?*

Q4 *Who are the key stakeholders for this issue? (This step is important. You need to know the audience for your analysis to help decide how to present your results.)*

Deliverables

After identifying the problem you're trying to solve, you need to envision the kinds of data displays (maps, graphics, and tables) that will address the problem. We recommend the following deliverables for this exercise:

1. A basemap showing Cook County and Chicago with census tracts from 2000. The map should show the population density classified in graduated color. Cook County and Chicago should be labeled.
2. A series of maps for 1990 and 2000 with normalized population data for African-Americans, Hispanics, and Caucasians. A short written analysis of spatial distribution of each ethnic group should be included on the map layout.
3. Maps showing diversity indexes in 1990 and 2000. The map should also show the percentage of African-American, Hispanic, Caucasian, and Asian populations as a bar graph.
4. A 3D representation of the 2000 Diversity Index.
5. A distribution analysis of median house values in 2000 for Chicago and Cook County.
6. A double variable map of diversity index in relation to median house value.
7. A double variable map of normalized African-American, Hispanic, or Caucasian data for 2000 shown in 3D in relation to median house value.

Examine the data

The next step in your workflow is to identify, collect, and examine the data for urban analysis. Here, we've identified and collected the data layers you will need. Explore the data to discover what information is contained in the layers.

You can use ArcCatalog to preview a GIS layer and explore the metadata associated with each feature class.

1. Open ArcCatalog and connect to the folder **OurWorld4\Module2\Project1\ data.**

2. Expand the data folder in the Catalog tree and double-click the Chicago geodatabase.

3. Click the Preview tab, then preview the geography and table for each feature class in the geodatabase.

The spatial coordinate system and the attributes are each important pieces of information about each data layer. You need this information for your analysis. Fortunately, the metadata associated with each layer allows you to access this information.

The Microsoft Excel database has been downloaded from http://factfinder.census.gov and technical documentation can be found at that link. The database can be opened in Microsoft Excel to preview the available attributes.

Q5 *Investigate the metadata and complete this table on your worksheet:*

Layer	Data Type	Publication Information: Who Created The Data?	Time Period Data Is Relevant	Spatial Horizontal Coordinate System	Attribute Values
chicago	Vector		2006		
county	Vector				
tracts_00			2006		
tracts_90		ESRI Data & Maps 2000		Geographic	

When you previewed tracts_00 and tracts_90, the geographic area that was displayed was a census tract. Census tracts are small, relatively permanent subdivisions of a county or city. (Read more about tracts at the Census Bureau's Web site, http://www.census.gov.)

> **Q6** *What information in tracts_00 and tracts_90 can be used to show possible residential patterns of African-Americans, Hispanics, and Caucasians?*

When you examine the data carefully, you will see that there are two populations given in tracts_00 and tracts_90. In tracts_00 the total population is given for 2000 and 2005. In tracts_90 the total population is given for 1990 and 1999. The 1999 and 2005 population values are only estimates of population and should not be used in calculations with the other attributes.

> **Q7** *Is there information in tracts_00 that can be used to display median house value?*

4. Close ArcCatalog.

Now that you've explored the available data, you're almost ready to begin your analysis. First you need to start a process summary, document your project, and set the project environments.

Organize and document your work

Step 1: Examine the directory structure

The next phase in a GIS project is to carefully keep track of the data and your calculations. You will work with a number of different files and it is important to keep them organized so you can easily find them. The best way to do this is to have a folder for your project that contains a data folder. For this project, the folder called **OurWorld4\Module2\Project1** will be your project folder. Make sure that it is stored in a place where you have write access. You can store your data inside the results folder. The results folder already contains an empty geodatabase named **project1_results.** Save your map documents inside the **OurWorld4\Module2\Project1\results** folder.

Step 2: Create a process summary

The process summary is just a list of the steps you used to do your analysis. We suggest using a simple text document for your process summary. Keep adding to it as you do your work to avoid forgetting any steps. The list below shows an example of the first few entries in a process summary:

1. Explore the data.
2. Produce a basemap showing Cook County and Chicago with census tracts from 2000.
3. Create maps for 1990 and 2000 with normalized population data for African-American, Hispanic, and Caucasian populations.

Step 3: Document the map

You need to add descriptive properties to every map document you produce. Use the same descriptive properties listed below for every map document in the module or individualize the documentation from map to map.

1. Open ArcMap and save the map document as **chicago1.** (Save it in the **OurWorld4\Module2\Project1\results** folder.)

2. From the File menu, choose Document Properties and in the dialog box add a title, author, and some descriptive text.

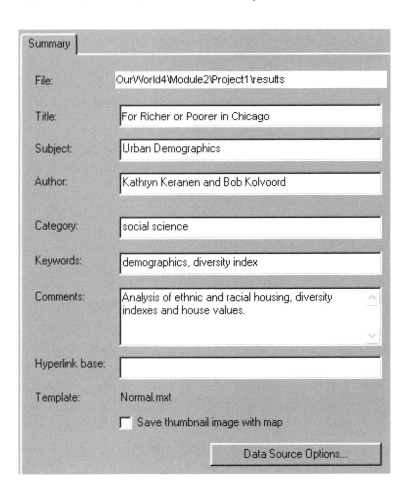

3. Click Data Source Options and then click the radio button to store relative paths of data sources. Click OK in both dialog boxes.

Storing data sources with relative paths allows ArcMap to automatically find all relevant data if you move your project folder to a new location or computer.

Step 4: Set the environments

In GIS analysis, you will often get data from several sources and this data may be in different coordinate systems and/or map projections. When using GIS to perform area calculations, you would like your result to be in familiar units, such as miles or kilometers. Data in an unprojected geographic coordinate system has units of decimal degrees, which are difficult to interpret. Thus, your calculations will be more meaningful if all the feature classes involved are in the same map projection. Fortunately, ArcMap can do much of this work for you if you set certain environment variables and data frame properties. In this section, you'll learn how to change these settings.

To display your data correctly, you'll need to set the coordinate system for the data frame. When you add data with a defined coordinate system, ArcMap will automatically set the data frame's projection to match the data. If you add subsequent layers that have a coordinate system different from the data frame, they are automatically projected on-the-fly to the data frame's coordinate system.

1. From the View menu, choose Data Frame Properties. Click the Coordinate System tab. Click Import. Navigate to your data folder, select tracts_00, and click Add. Click OK.

Before using ArcToolbox tools to make your calculations, you will establish some general environment settings that apply to all of the tools you'll be using. The analysis environment includes the workspace where results will be placed, and the extent, cell size, and coordinate system of the results.

2. Open ArcToolbox, right-click any empty space within ArcToolbox and choose Environments.

3. Expand General Settings

By default, inputs and outputs are placed in your current workspace, but you can redirect the output to another workspace such as your results folder.

4. Set the Current Workspace as **OurWorld4\Module2\Project1\data.**

5. Set the Scratch Workspace as **OurWorld4\Module2\Project1\results\ project1_results.gdb.**

6. For Output Coordinate System select "Same as Display."

7. For Extent select "Same as Display."

8. Click OK.

9. Save the map document as **chicago1.**

Analysis

Once you've examined the data, completed map documentation, and set the environments, you are ready to begin the analysis and to complete the displays you need to address the problem. A good place to start any GIS analysis is to produce a basemap to better understand the distribution of features in the geographic area you're studying. First, you will prepare a basemap showing Chicago and Cook County. You will include the 2000 census tracts displayed by population density on your basemap.

Step 1: Create a basemap of Cook County

The basemap should show Cook County and Chicago with census tracts from 2000. The map should show the population density classified in graduated color. Cook County and Chicago should be labeled.

1. Add tracts_00 and symbolize it by Quantities/Graduated Color using the POP00_SQMI field.

2. Click OK.

3. Add Chicago and make it hollow so you can see just the city outline overlaid on the Cook County census tracts.

4. Label Cook County and Chicago with callout labels.

A callout label is a dramatic style that provides a box around the label text and a connecting line (leader line) to the feature being labeled. It is like a thought balloon in a cartoon.

5. Save the map document.

Q8 *Describe the spatial distribution of population in Cook County.*

▶ Deliverable 1: A basemap showing Cook County and Chicago with census tracts from 2000. The map should show the population density classified in graduated color. Cook County and Chicago should be labeled.

Step 2: Compare race/ethnicity for 1990 and 2000

1. Open a new map document and save it as **chicago2.mxd.**

2. Refer back to "Organize and document your work" and do the following:

    a. *Document the map.*

    b. *Set the data frame properties. Data frame properties must be set for each data frame.*

    c. *Set the environments.*

3. Rename the data frame **percentage African-American.**

41

4. Add tracts_90.

To compare data, set a standard classification that can be used for both datasets. This can be done by creating a layer definition and applying it to both the 1990 and 2000 data.

5. Create the layer definition:

   a. *Display tracts_90 using Quantities/Graduated Color with Black (African-American) as the Value field and normalizing by POP1990.*

   b. *Click Classify and select Manual for the Classification Method.*

   c. *In the Break Value box type in the values of **0.2, 0.4, 0.6, 0.8,** and leave the last value as 1.0.*

   d. *Click OK.*

   e. *Click Label and go to Format Labels.*

   f. *Under Category, choose Percentage and click the radio button for "The number represents a fraction. Adjust it to show a percentage."*

   g. *Click Numeric Options and round the number of decimal places to 1.*

   h. *Click OK. Click OK.*

   i. *Right-click tracts_90 and save as a layer file. Name the layer file **comparison**. This layer file will be used as the standard with which to compare the other layers.*

6. Add tracts_00 and display using quantities/graduated color with Black as the Value field and normalizing by POP2000.

7. Go to Symbology and click Import. Import the comparison layer file you saved above.

8. Click OK.

9. Change the Normalization Field to POP2000.

10. Click OK. Click OK.

11. Add Chicago and make it hollow.

12. Compare the data using one of these methods:

   a. *Turn tracts_00 on and off.*

   b. *Turn on the Effects toolbar.*

      i. Choose Layer tracts_00 in the Effects toolbar and click the Swipe tool. Swipe north to south or east to west by clicking and dragging your cursor vertically or horizontally.

      ii. Select Flicker Layer to flicker between the layers.

M ● ● ○ ○ ○
P ● ○ ○

Q9 *Why should you normalize the data?*

Q10 *How does the normalized data differ from the original data?*

Q11 *Describe the distribution of the African-American population and how it has changed between 1990 and 2000.*

13. Right-click the Percentage of African-Americans Data Frame and select Copy.

14. From the Edit menu, click Paste. Change the duplicate African-Americans data frame name to **percentage Hispanics.**

15. Import the comparison layer file that you are using as the standard symbolization and change the value field from **Black** to **Hispanic.** Make the Normalization Field match either the 1990 or 2000 layer, respectively.

Q12 *Describe the distribution of the Hispanic population and how it has changed between 1990 and 2000.*

16. Repeat the process for Caucasians (use the data in the White field).

Q13 *Describe the distribution of the Caucasian population and how it has changed between 1990 and 2000.*

17. Create a layout showing the percentage of African-Americans, Hispanics, and Caucasians in 2000.

18. Save your map document as **chicago2.**

▶ Deliverable 2: A series of maps for 1990 and 2000 with normalized population data for African-Americans, Hispanics, and Caucasians. A short written analysis of spatial distribution of each ethnic group should be included on the map.

Step 3: Calculate and display Cook County diversity index for 1999 and 2000

USA Today worked with some college professors to develop a diversity index to represent racial and ethnic diversity with a single number. The first diversity index was created in 1991 and then updated for 2000. In this step, you will calculate the diversity index for 1990 and 2000, make observations about diversity in Cook County, and compare diversity in 1990 with that observed in 2000. Consult the following Web site for more background on the diversity index: http://www.unc.edu/~pmeyer/carstat/tools.html.

A. Calculate and study diversity index for 2000

1. Open a new map document and save it as **chicago3.mxd.**

2. Refer back to "Organize and document your work" and do the following:

   a. *Document the map.*

   b. *Set the data frame properties. They must be set for each data frame.*

   c. *Set the environments.*

3. Add tracts_00.

4. Export the data into the project1_results geodatabase in the results folder and name it **tracts_00_DI.** Save the file as a "File and Personal Geodatabase feature class."

5. Remove tracts_00.

6. Open the attribute table of tracts_00_DI.

7. This attribute table is extremely long, and since you are only dealing with population, hide the other fields by holding down the control key and double-clicking the field headers for age, households, families and housing units, sex, area and the population for 2005, state_fips, cnty_fips, stcofips, and tract. The following fields should still be visible: OBJECTID, Shape, FIPS, POP2000, WHITE, BLACK, AMERI_ES, ASIAN, HAWN_PI, OTHER, MULTI_RACE, AND HISPANIC.

8. Save the map document.

9. Add the following fields (make the type of each field "float" and accept the default Field Properties):
   per_white
   per_black
   per_ameri_es
   per_asian
   per_hawnpi
   per_other
   per_hisp
   per_Nhisp
   div_index

10. Next, calculate the percentage of each of the races and ethnic groups as follows (due to the nature of the 1990 data—some of the census blocks have no reported population—and the fact that you can't divide by zero, the data has to be slightly edited):

    a. *Select by attributes POP2000>0.*

    b. *Right-click the field header per_white, go to Field Calculator and enter the following formula: WHITE/POP2000*

Module 2: Project 1

c. *Click OK.*

d. *If you examine the data, you can see that some of the field values are <NULL>. The <NULL> values need to be set to 0. Go to Options at the bottom of the attribute table and select "Switch Selection."*

e. *Right-click the field header per_white, select the Field Calculator and enter **0** as the value instead of WHITE/POP2000. Click OK. This changes all the <NULL> values to 0.*

11. Repeat the previous step for per_black, per_ameri_es, per_asian, per_hawnpi, per_other and per_hisp. (In each category, first select the POP2000>0.)

12. For the field per_Nhisp, use the Field Calculator and enter **1-per_hisp.** Be sure to Clear Selected Features before performing the calculation.

13. To calculate the diversity index (div_index), use the Field Calculator and enter the following formula: **1 - ([per_white]^2 + [per_black]^2+ [per_ameri_es]^2+ [per_asian]^2 + [per_hawnpi]^2 + [per_other]^2) * ([per_hisp]^2+ [per_Nhisp]^2)**
(Note: MULTI_RACE is not included.)

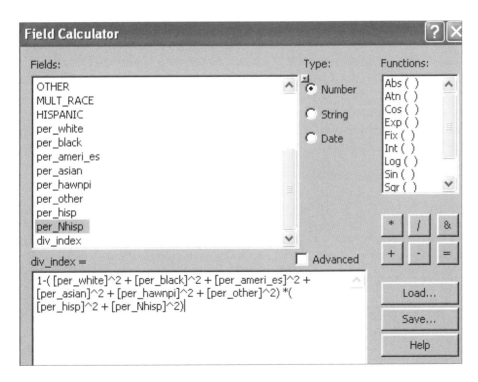

14. Display div_index in graduated colors and exclude values of 1 (Hint: You can exclude values by clicking the Classify button in the Symbology tab, then clicking Exclusion in the Query tab and entering "div_index"=1).

15. Create a layer file to use for comparing the diversity index in different years. Symbolize by Manual with 4 classes. For Break Values, enter **0.2, 0.4, 0.6,** and leave the last value as is. Format the labels to two decimal places.

16. Save the layer file as **div_index.**

Q14 *Where are there clusters of high and low diversity?*

Q15 *What does low diversity mean?*

17. Save the map document.

B. Calculate and study diversity index for 1990

The Census race/ethnic group definitions changed a bit between 1990 and 2000, so you'll need to use a slightly different formula to calculate the 1990 diversity index.

1. Add tracts_90.

2 Export the data into the results folder and name it **tracts_90_DI.**

3. Remove tracts_90.

4. Open the attribute table for tracts_90_DI.

5. This attribute table is extremely long. Since you are only dealing with population, hide the other fields by holding down the control key and double-clicking the field headers for age, households, families and housing units, sex, area and the population for 1999, state_fips, cnty_fips, stcofips and tract. The following fields should still be visible: ObjectID, Shape, FIPS, POP1990, WHITE, BLACK, AMERI_ES, ASIAN_PI, OTHER, AND HISPANIC.

6. Save the map document.

7. Add the following fields (make the type of each field "float" and accept the default Field Properties).
per_white
per_black
per_ameri_es
per_asian_pi
per_other
per_hisp
per_Nhisp
div_index

8. Now you have to calculate the percentage for each of the races and ethnic groups.

Due to the nature of the 1990 data (some of the census blocks have no reported population) and the fact that you can't divide by zero, the data has to be slightly edited:

    a. *Select by attributes with POP1990>0.*

    b. *Right-click the field header per_white, select Field Calculator and enter the following formula:* **WHITE/POP1990**

    c. *Click OK.*

    d. *If you examine the data, some of the field values are <NULL>. The <NULL> values need to be 0. Go to Options at the bottom of the attribute table and select "Switch Selection."*

    e. *Right-click the field header per_white, select the Field Calculator and enter* **0** *as the value instead of WHITE/POP1990. Click OK. This changes all the <NULL> values to 0.*

    f. *Click OK.*

9. Repeat the previous step for per_black, per_ameri_es, per_asian_pi, per_other and per_hisp. (In each category, first select the POP1990>0.)

10. For the field per_Nhisp, use the Field Calculator and enter **1-per_hisp.** Be sure to Clear Selected Features before performing the calculation.

11. To calculate the div_index, use the Field Calculator and enter the following formula: **1-([per_white]^2+ [per_black]^2+ [per_ameri_es]^2+ [per_asian_pi]^2+ [per_other]^2) * ([per_hisp]^2 + [per_Nhisp]^2).**

12. Symbolize div_index by importing the div_index layer file.

(Q16) *Where are there clusters of high and low diversity?*

13. Move tracts_90_DI to the bottom of the table of contents.

14. Save the map document.

15. Compare the 2000 diversity index to the 1990 diversity index. You can do this by turning the layers on and off, or using the Effects toolbar and swiping or blinking the layers.

16. Save the map document.

(Q17) *Describe how the diversity index has changed from 1990 to 2000.*

Step 4: Examine diversity of individual census tracts

In the next part of the exercise, you will look at the diversity of individual census blocks.

1. Copy the layer tracts_00_DI and paste.

2. Display the new layer by Bar/Column with Whites, Blacks, Asians and Hispanics normalized with POP2000. Uncheck prevent chart overlap. Make the background color hollow. Click Size and select 30. Click Properties and uncheck Show Leader Lines.

Q18 *Closely investigate Cook County by zooming in. What do you observe about the diversity of the census tracts?*

3. Save the map document.

▶ Deliverable 3: Maps showing diversity indexes of 1990 and 2000. The map should also show the percentage of African-American, Hispanic, Caucasian, and Asian population as a bar graph.

Hint: Remember to make a layout showing multiple maps, you must insert a new Data Frame for each map. In order to create Deliverable 3 you must insert separate Data Frames for Diversity Index 1990, Diversity Index 2000, and Individual Census tracts.

Step 5: Display the data in 3D

Now, you will use ArcScene, the 3D visualization application that allows you to view your GIS data in three dimensions and to overlay many layers of data in a 3D environment.

1. Open ArcScene and add tracts_00_DI.

2. Refer back to "Organize and document your work" and do the following:

   a. *Document the map.*

   b. *Set the data frame properties (In ArcScene, right click Scene Layers and choose Scene Properties).*

3. Right-click tracts_00_DI and select Properties. Click the Extrusion tab.

4. Click the Expression Builder icon to the right of the Extrusion value box and select div_index as the expression. Click OK. Click OK.

5. Right-click Scene layers and select Scene Properties. Click the General tab and then click Calculate From Extent to have the computer calculate the appropriate vertical exaggeration. Click OK.

6. Import the div_index layer file.

7. Save the map document as chicago_di.

48

(Q19) *What does looking at the data in 3D reveal?*

▶ **Deliverable 4: A 3D representation of the 2000 Diversity Index.**

Step 6: Analyze distribution and change in median house values

In this step, data preparation requires an Internet connection, an Internet browser, and Microsoft Excel software.

Many factors can affect diversity in an urban setting, but economics is one of the most powerful. House values as an economic indicator help you understand the changing patterns of diversity. Think about other indicators you might use to explore this problem.

You discovered earlier that tracts_00 did not have a median house value attribute. To compare median house value in 1990 and 2000 you must obtain that data from another source. You can download median house value data from http://factfinder.census.gov as a Microsoft Excel worksheet. The worksheet will have to be modified before it can be used in your geospatial analysis.

A. Download the data from U.S. Census Bureau

1. Using your Internet browser, go to http://factfinder.census.gov.

2. On the left side of the page, click DATA SETS.

3. Under the heading 2000, click the radio button beside Census 2000 Summary File 3 (SF 3) – Sample Data.

4. After checking the radio button, click Detailed Tables.

5. Under Select a geographic type, select State…County…Census Tract.

6. Under Select a State, choose Illinois.

7. Under Select a County, choose Cook County.

8. Under Select one or more geographic areas, choose All Census Tracts. Don't forget to click Add.

9. When all the census tracts populate the Current geography selections, click Next.

10. The table that shows Median House value is H76, Median Value (Dollars) for Specified Owner-Occupied Housing Units. Choose that table and click Add.

11. Click Show Result.

12. Find the Print/Download tab at the top of the page. Click Download. Note: "Automatic prompting for file downloads" must be enabled on Internet Explorer to ensure a complete download of census tract data. For further assistance, click Download and click the link "Using FactFinder with Windows XP SP2."

13. In the window that appears, scroll down and click the radio button next to Microsoft Excel (.xls).

14. Click OK and save the downloaded file to the **OurWorld4/Module2/ Project1/Results** folder.

15. Unzip the data.

B. Clean up the data

1. Double-click dt_dec_2000_sf3_u_data1.xls and the spreadsheet will open in Excel. Verify that you have downloaded thousands of records, not just a few.

2. To solve the missing median house value data in the tract_00 feature class, you only require two columns from the table. Delete all the other columns except the following:

   • *11- DIGIT Geography Identifier, which is actually the FIPS number (Federal Information Processing Standard)*

   • *Specified owner_occupied housing units: Median value*

3. Delete the first Row.

4. Change the header of the Geography Identifier column to FIPS and the header of the Specified owner-occupied housing units: Median value to median_val. Change the Row Height of the first row to 15.

	A	B
1	FIPS	Median_val
2	17031000000	0
3	17031010100	187500
4	17031010200	145200
5	17031010300	172200
6	17031010400	156300
7	17031010500	236100
8	17031010600	191800

5. Save the spreadsheet to OurWorld4/Module2/Project1/Results as house_val. This file will be used for later analysis.

In order to use this data, you need to join it to census tracts 2000.

C. Prepare the map

1. Open a new map document and save it as **chicago4.mxd.**

2. Refer back to "Organize and document your work" and do the following:

    a. *Document the map.*

    b. *Set the data frame properties. They must be set for each data frame.*

    c. *Set the environments.*

3. Add tracts_00.

4. Add the spreadsheet file house_val. To do this, you must double-click house_val so that Sheet0$ appears. Add Sheet0$ to the table of contents.

5. Right-click tracts_00, select Join and Relates, and then select Join.

6. Choose FIPS as the field in this layer upon which the join will be based.

7. The software should automatically identify the spreadsheet Sheet0$ as the table to join and FIPS as the field to use to join to the tracts_00 feature class.

8. Click OK.

You need to get rid of any of the tracts that did not join with the census data (NULL data) and then you want to export the file so that it becomes permanent.

9. Open the tracts_00 table.

10. You need to select all the values that are NOT 0 or <NULL>. Go to Selection by Attribute and select "median_val" > 0.

11. Close the attribute table.

12. Right-click tracts_00 and select Data/Export.

13. Save the file as tracts_00_2.

14. Remove house_val and tracts_00.

15. Display tracts_00_2 by Quantities using the value field median_val.

16. You need to reformat the legend to eliminate the extraneous digits to the right of the decimal point. Right-click tracts_00_2 and choose Properties/Symbology.

17. Click Label (below the Color Ramp menu) and Select Format Label.

18. Change the Number of decimal places to 0.

19. Click OK. Click OK.

20. Add Chicago and make it hollow.

21. Save the map document.

Q20 *What does the median value represent?*

Q21 *What is the lowest median_val?*

Q22 *What is the highest median_val?*

Q23 *Describe the spatial distribution of house values in Cook County.*

▶ Deliverable 5: A distribution analysis of median house values in 2000 for Chicago and Cook County.

Step 7: Create a histogram of median house values in 2000

1. Select the houses with median values >0.

2. Save as **tracts_00_3** in your results folder.

3. Remove tracts_00_2.

4. Select Tools/Graphs and choose Create to open the graphing wizard.

5. Set the graph type to histogram, the Layer/Table to tracts_00_3, and the value field to median_val.

6. Click Next and title the graph **Distribution of Median House Values.** Click Finish.

Q24 *What does Count on y-axis represent?*

Q25 *What does the median_val on the x-axis represent?*

7. Save the map document.

The graph is dynamically linked to the map. As you click a histogram bar, the census blocks with median house values in that range are highlighted on the map. Starting at the left (lowest house value), click each section of the histogram. Observe the spatial patterns on the map.

Q26 *Explain the patterns that you see.*

Step 8: Prepare a double variable map showing the relation between diversity index and median house value

1. Open ArcMap and Add tracts_00_DI.

2. Refer back to "Organize and document your work" and do the following:

   a. *Document the map.*

   b. *Set the data frame properties.*

3. Add house_val.

4. Right-click tracts_00_DI and join to house_val by FIPS.

5. Right-click and go to Data/Export data and save the file as **tractsdi_val.**

You now have one feature class with the diversity index and the median house value included. You do not have to save the project.

6. Open ArcScene.

7. Refer back to "Organize and document your work" and do the following:

   • *Document the map.*

   • *Set the data frame properties. They must be set for each data frame. (In ArcScene, right-click Scene Layers and choose Scene Properties.)*

8. Add tractsdi_val.

9. Display by quantities using the median_val field. Exclude 0.

10. Right-click tractsdi_val, choose Properties, click the Extrusion tab, and extrude by the diversity index.

11. Right-click Scene Layers, choose Properties, and click the General Tab. Click Calculate from Extent to calculate the vertical exaggeration.

12. Save the project as **chicagodi_hval.**

Q27 *Explain the double variable map.*

▶ Deliverable 6: A double variable map of diversity index in relation to median house value.

Step 9: Prepare 3D race/ethnicity maps relating to 2000 house values

1. Open ArcScene and add tracts_00_2.

2. Refer back to "Organize and document your work" and do the following:

   a. *Document the map.*

   b. *Set the data frame properties. (In ArcScene, right-click Scene Layers and choose Scene Properties.)*

3. Symbolize tracts_00_2 by importing the comparison.lyr file. Select Black and change the Normalization Field to POP2000. Click OK.

4. Right-click tracts_00_2 and go to Properties.

5. Click the Extrusion tab.

6. Click the Expression Builder icon to the right of the Extrusion value box and select MEDIAN_VAL as the expression.

7. Click OK. Click OK.

This extrudes the polygons by the median house value. The vertical exaggeration of the feature needs to be defined to fit the values to the display.

8. Right-click Scene Layers and click the General Tab. Click Calculate from Extent to calculate the vertical exaggeration.

9. Click OK.

10. Repeat step 3 only for Caucasian and Hispanic population percentages and observe their variations with respect to the extruded median house value.

This kind of display is a called a double variable map because you're able to explore two variables at the same time. This type of map is a very powerful analysis tool.

Q28 *Describe the relationship between median house value and the concentrations of different ethnic/racial groups.*

Q29 *What other variables might you analyze to understand the changing patterns of diversity in Chicago?*

▶ **Deliverable 7: A double variable map of normalized African-American, Hispanic, and Caucasian data for 2000 shown in 3D in relation to median house value.**

Once your analysis is complete, you're not done. You still need to develop a solution to the original problem and present your results in a compelling way to the local university in this particular situation. The presentation of your various data displays must explain what they show and how they contribute to solving the problem.

Presentation

Write a report documenting your analysis explaining the spatial patterns you observed. Remember that your audience probably lacks your in-depth knowledge of GIS, so you'll need to communicate your results in a way that they'll be able to understand and use.

Extending the project

Your instructor may choose for you to complete this optional exercise.

Explore other demographic attributes

There are many other demographic avenues to explore. Conduct an analysis of age groups (Age_65_up and Age_under5). Examine the percentage of males and females. Analyze vacant housing. Calculate the diversity index by school zones or congressional districts.

Determining diversity in Washington, D.C.

Scenario

Washington, D.C., is an economically and ethnically diverse community with interesting patterns of settlement and change. A public policy think tank is studying the changes in the nation's capital during the 1990s. It is interested in the spatial distribution of the residences of African-Americans, Caucasians, and Hispanics and the spatial distribution of median house value in the year 2000.

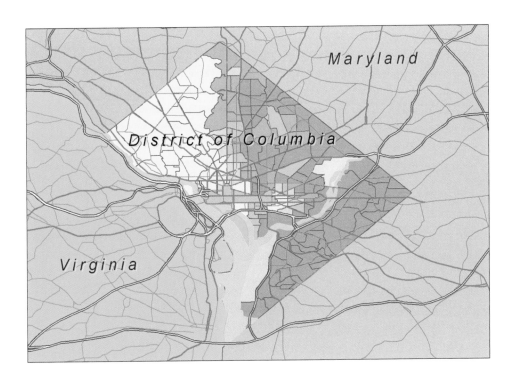

Problem

The think tank has contracted with you to make maps, charts, and graphs of residential patterns and median house value to use in its research.

Reminder

It helps to divide a large problem such as this into a set of smaller tasks such as the following:

1. Identify the geographic study area.
2. Determine the sequence of steps in your study.
3. Identify the decisions to be made.
4. Develop the information required to make decisions.
5. Identify stakeholders for this issue.

Deliverables

We recommend the following deliverables for this problem:

1. A basemap showing Washington, D.C., with census tracts from 2000. The map should show the population density classified in graduated color.
   You can add the layers mjr_hwys and dtl_water to give you a basis from which to write descriptive narratives of the population density's spatial patterns.
2. A series of maps for 1990 and 2000 with normalized population data for African-American, Hispanic, and Caucasian residents displayed for each census tract. A short written analysis of spatial distribution of each ethnic group should be included on the map layout.
3. Maps showing diversity indexes of 1990 and 2000. The map should also show the percentage of Caucasian, African-American, Asian, and Hispanic population as a bar graph.
4. A 3D representation of the 2000 Diversity Index.
5. A distribution analysis of median house values in 2000 for Washington, D.C.
6. A double variable map of diversity index in relation to median house value.
7. A double variable map of normalized African-American, Caucasian, or Hispanic data for 2000 shown in 3D in relation to median house value.

Examine the data

The data for this project is stored in the **OurWorld4\Module2\Project2\data** folder.

Reminder

You can explore the metadata in ArcCatalog. The table below helps you organize this information.

Q1 *Investigate the metadata and complete this table on your worksheet:*

Layer	Data Type	Publication Information: Who Created The Data?	Time Period Data Is Relevant	Spatial Horizontal Coordinate System	Attribute Values
dc	Vector		2006		
tracts_00			2006		
tracts_90		ESRI Data & Maps 2000		Geographic	

Organize and document your work

Reminder

Be sure to refer to the module 2, project 1 exercise and your process summary.

2000 Diversity Index = 1-([per_white]^2 + [per_black]^2 + [per_ameri_es]^2 + [per_asian]^2 + [per_hawnpi]^2 + [per_other]^2) * ([per_hisp]^2 + [per_Nhisp]^2)

Note: MULTI_RACE is not included.

1990 Diversity Index = 1- ([per_white]^2 + [per_black]^2 + [per_ameri_es]^2 + [per_asian_pi]^2 + [per_other]^2) * ([per_hisp]^2 + [per_Nhisp]^2])

Analysis

An important first step in GIS analysis is to develop a basemap of your study area.

Complete deliverable 1 and answer the questions below to orient yourself to the study area.

▶ **Deliverable 1: A basemap showing Washington, D.C., with census tracts from 2000. The map should show the population density classified in graduated color. You can add the layers mjr_hwys and dtl_water to give you a basis from which to write descriptive narratives of the population density's spatial patterns.**

Q2 *Write a paragraph describing the spatial distribution of population in Washington, D.C. (The river on the western side of Washington, D.C., is the Potomac River. Constitution and Independence avenues are the major streets that go west to east and meet at the Capitol. Georgia Avenue runs north to south.)*

To complete deliverable 2, you need to make an appropriate legend. Create a layer file using tracts_90 displayed in graduated color with whites as the Value field and normalizing by POP1990. The manual breaks should be set to 0.2, 0.4, 0.6, 0.8, and 1.19. Be sure to format the labels correctly and then use the layer file as the standard display scheme.

▶ **Deliverable 2: A series of maps for 1990 and 2000 with normalized population data for African-American, Hispanic, and Caucasian residents. A short written analysis should be included on the map layout.**

Q3 *Describe the changes in population for each race/ethnic group between 1990 and 2000.*

▶ **Deliverable 3: Maps showing diversity indexes of 1990 and 2000. The map should also show the percentage of African-American, Hispanic, Caucasian, and Asian population as a bar graph.**

Reminder

Be sure to refer to the module 2, project 1 exercise and your process summary.

Q4 *Where are there clusters of high diversity?*

Q5 *Describe how the diversity index has changed from 1990 to 2000.*

▶ **Deliverable 4: A 3D representation of the 2000 Diversity Index.**

Reminder

This deliverable requires ArcScene, the 3D viewing application. You need to extrude by the diversity index and then let the computer calculate the correct vertical exaggeration.

Before completing deliverable 5, you must download and clean up the census data for median house value of 2000. Refer to your process summary if you forget any of the steps.

▶ **Deliverable 5: An analysis of the spatial distribution of median house values in 2000.**

Reminder

Save the file as tracts_00_2 after you have joined the median house value data.

Q6 *Describe the spatial distribution of median house values in 2000.*

▶ **Deliverable 6: A double variable map of diversity index in relation to median house value.**

Reminder

Deliverables 6 and 7 require that you use ArcScene in the 3D Analyst extension. Set the vertical exaggeration after you extrude.

▶ **Deliverable 7: A double variable map of normalized African-American, Caucasian, and Hispanic data for 2000 shown in 3D in relation to median house value.**

Presentation

Remember to keep in mind the interests and expertise of your audience as you prepare your presentation. Remember to develop a solution to the original problem and present your results in a compelling way.

Extending the project

Your instructor may choose for you to answer the following questions.

Q7 *How do the distributions of African-Americans, Caucasians, Hispanics, and median house values compare to the Chicago area?*

Q8 *How does the diversity index compare to Chicago?*

Module 2: Project 3 ● ● ○

On your own

You've worked through a guided activity examining variation in the diversity index in an urban area and you've downloaded additional data and repeated that analysis. In this section you will reinforce the skills you've developed by researching and analyzing a similar scenario, but this time entirely on your own. One of the first challenges is that you must identify your study area and acquire the data you need for your analysis. We suggest several possible demographic scales below. However, if there is another scale that has significant interest to you, download and work with that data.

Possible scales:
a. Urban areas of your state
b. City boundaries
c. School districts
d. Congressional districts
e. Counties

Refer to your process summary and the preceding module activities if you need help. We've outlined some basic steps to help you organize your work.

Research

Research the problem and answer the following questions before you begin:

1. What is the area of study?
2. What is the interest in this area and who are the stakeholders?

Obtain the data

Do you have access to baseline data? The ESRI Data and Maps Media Kit provides many of the layers of data that are needed for project work. Be sure to pay particular attention to the source of data and get the latest version. Older versions of the ESRI Data and Maps Media Kit are very useful for temporal comparison—be sure to check the date.

If you do not have access to The ESRI Data and Maps Media Kit, data can be obtained from the following sources:

- http://www.esri.com/tiger—*Baseline data from the 1990 and 2000 Census can be found here.*
- http://geographynetwork.com
- http://www.nationalatlas.gov

Workflow

After researching the problem and obtaining the data you should do the following:

1. Write a brief scenario.
2. State the problem.
3. Define the deliverables.
4. Examine the data using ArcCatalog.
5. Set the directory structure, start your legacy file, and document the map.
6. Decide what you need for the Data Frame Coordinate System and the Environments.
   a. What is the best projection for your work?
   b. Do you need to set a cell size or mask?
7. Start your analysis.
8. Prepare your presentation and deliverables

Always remember to document your work in a process summary.

M ● ● ○ ○ ○
P ● ● ●

MODULE 3

Law enforcement decisions

Introduction

A geospatial approach to crime fighting helps decision makers deploy limited police resources—personnel, equipment, facilities—for maximum benefit. In this module, we focus on law enforcement in Houston, Texas, and Lincoln, Nebraska, two cities that have successfully incorporated GIS technology into their crime analysis and planning processes. You have the opportunity to use actual data to size up the crime situation in each city and recommend specific action plans based on your GIS analysis. This module uses buffer zones, geocoding, and mapping density. The maps you produce will be the type of effective visual representations that, in the real world, assist decision makers and inform citizens.

Projects in this module:

- **Taking a bite out of Houston's crime**

- **Logging Lincoln's police activity**

- **On your own**

Module worksheets

The student worksheet files can be found on the Data and Resources DVD.

Project 1 student sheet

- File name: Houston_student_worksheet.doc
- Location: OurWorld4\Module3\Project1\documents
- Document length: 7 pages
- Worksheet for "Taking a bite out of Houston's crime." A form for answering questions, completing tables, and tracking work to be handed in.

Project 2 student sheet

- File name: Lincoln_student_worksheet.doc
- Location: OurWorld4\Module3\Project2\documents
- Document length: 5 pages
- Worksheet for "Logging Lincoln's police activity." A form for answering questions, completing tables, and tracking work to be handed in.

Taking a bite out of Houston's crime

Scenario

Law enforcement agencies increasingly are adopting GIS as a tool to improve public safety. Officials can decide where and how to allocate their resources once they pinpoint crime clusters. Spatial data helps police explore various factors contributing to crime.

In this exercise you will use data from the City of Houston to perform a crime analysis. The data comes from the Positive Interaction Program (PIP), commonly called the PIP Crime Bulletin.

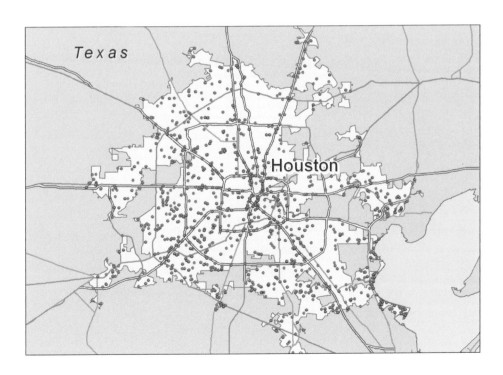

Problem

The Houston Police Department has the technology available for crime analysis to allocate patrol resources efficiently. Imagine that you are a department GIS analyst who has been directed to investigate the following:

- Crime patterns in proximity to police stations to determine if current patrols are effective or adjustments are necessary, such as reorganizing beats and building new substations.
- Patterns of aggravated assault, burglary, and narcotics-related crimes.
- Patterns of when crimes are committed.

In applying GIS to a problem, you must have a very clear understanding of the problem or scenario. We find it helpful to answer these four questions, which test your understanding and divide the problem into a set of smaller problems that are easier to solve.

Q1 *What geographic area are you studying? (Record answers on your worksheet.)*

Q2 *What decision do you need to make?*

Q3 *What information would help you make the decision?*

Q4 *Who are the key stakeholders for this issue? (This step is important. You need to know the audience for your analysis to help decide how to present your results.)*

Deliverables

After identifying the problem you're trying to solve, you need to envision the kinds of data displays (maps, graphs, and tables) that will address the problem. We recommend the following deliverables for this exercise:

1. A basemap of Houston showing police stations, crimes, and roads. Include a graph of total crimes.
2. A map of police stations and locations of crimes along with recommendations for new police substation sites.
3. Density maps of aggravated assault, burglary, and narcotics-related crimes.
4. A graph exploring the time of day crimes are committed.

Examine the data

The next step in your workflow is to identify, collect, and examine the data. Here, we've identified and collected the data layers you will need. Explore the data to discover what information is contained in the various layers.

You can use ArcCatalog to preview the GIS data and explore the metadata associated with each feature class.

1. Open ArcCatalog and connect to the folder **OurWorld4\Module3\Project1\data.**

2. Expand the data folder in the Catalog tree and double-click the Houston geodatabase.

3. Click the Preview tab, then preview the geography and table for each feature class in the geodatabase.

Q5 *Investigate the metadata and complete this table on your worksheet:*

Layer	Data Type	Publication Information: Who Created The Data?	Time Period Data Is Relevant	Spatial Horizontal Coordinate System	Attribute Values
aug06.xls	Excel worksheet	http://www.houstontx.gov/police/stats.htm	2006	N/A	
blkgrp					
houston			2003		Census Data
usa_sts		Tele Atlas North America, Inc., ESRI		Geographic	Street Data

4. Close ArcCatalog.

Now that you've explored the available data, you're almost ready to begin your analysis. First you need to start a process summary, document your project, and set the project environments.

Organize and document your work

Step 1: Examine the directory structure

The next phase in a GIS project is to carefully keep track of the data and your calculations. You will work with a number of different files and it is important to keep them organized so you can easily find them. The best way to do this is to have a folder for your project that contains a data folder. For this project, the folder called **OurWorld4\Module3\Project1\results** will be your project folder. Make sure that it is stored in a place where you have write access. You can store your data inside the results folder. The results folder already contains an empty geodatabase named **project1_results.** Save your map documents inside the **OurWorld4\Module3\Project1\results** folder.

Step 2: Create a process summary

The process summary is just a list of the steps you used to do your analysis. We suggest a simple text document for your process summary. Keep adding to it as you do your work to avoid forgetting any steps. The list below shows an example of the first few entries in a process summary:

1. Explore the data.
2. Produce a basemap of the Houston area showing police stations, crimes, and roads. Include a graph of total crime.
3. Produce a map of police stations and locations of crimes.

Step 3: Document the map

You need to add descriptive properties to every map document you produce. Use the same descriptive properties listed below for every map document in the module or individualize the documentation from map to map.

1. Open ArcMap and save the map document as **crime.** (Save it in the **OurWorld4\Module3\Project1\results** folder.)

2. From the File menu, choose Document Properties and in the dialog box add a title, author, and some descriptive text.

Title:	Taking a Bite out of Houston's Crime
Subject:	Crime Analysis
Author:	Kathryn Keranen and Bob Kolvoord
Category:	Crime Analysis
Keywords:	density maps, temporal study, animation, proximity
Comments:	Crime statistics from the City of Houston are geocoded and analyzed using various GIS techniques of density and proximity.
Hyperlink base:	
Template:	Normal.mxt

☐ Save thumbnail image with map

Data Source Options...

3. Click Data Source Options and then click the radio button to store relative paths of data sources. Click OK in both dialog boxes.

Storing data sources with relative paths allows ArcMap to automatically find all relevant data if you move your project folder to a new location or computer.

Step 4: Set the environments

In GIS analysis, you will often get data from several sources and this data may be in different coordinate systems and/or map projections. When using GIS to perform area calculations, you would like your result to be in familiar units, such as miles or kilometers. Data in an unprojected geographic coordinate system has units of decimal degrees, which are difficult to interpret. Thus, your calculations will be more meaningful if all the feature classes involved are in the same map projection. Fortunately, ArcMap can do much of this work for you if you set certain environment variables and data frame properties. In this step, you'll learn how to change these settings.

To display your data correctly, you'll need to set the coordinate system for the data frame. When you add data with a defined coordinate system, ArcMap will automatically set the data frame's projection to match the data. If you add subsequent layers that have a coordinate system different from the data frame, they are automatically projected on-the-fly to the data frame's coordinate system.

1. From the View menu, choose Data Frame Properties. Click the Coordinate System tab. Expand Predefined, expand Projected Coordinate Systems, expand UTM, expand NAD 1983, and select Zone 15N. Click OK.

2. Add the Houston feature class from the Houston.gdb. Click Close in the Geographic Coordinate Systems Warning window. (Note: Remember to do this any time this warning dialog box appears.)

Before using ArcToolbox tools to make your calculations, you will establish some general environment settings that apply to all of the tools you'll be using. The analysis environment includes the workspace where results will be placed, and the extent, cell size, and coordinate system for the results.

3. Open ArcToolbox, right-click any empty space within ArcToolbox, and choose Environments.

4. Expand General Settings.

By default, inputs and outputs are placed in your current workspace, but you can redirect the output to another workspace such as your results folder.

5. Set the Current Workspace as **OurWorld4\Module3\Project1\data.**

6. Set the Scratch Workspace as **OurWorld4\Module3\Project1\results\ project1_results.gdb.**

7. For the Output Coordinate System, select "Same as Display."

8. For Extent, select "Same as layer Houston."

9. Expand Raster Analysis Settings.

10. Set the Cell size to 200.

You also want to limit your analysis to the city of Houston. This is accomplished by using an analysis mask. The mask identifies those locations within the analysis extent that will be included when using a tool.

11. Set the Mask to Houston.

12. Click OK.

13. Save the map document as **crime1.**

Analysis

Once you've examined the data, completed map documentation, and set the environments, you are ready to begin the analysis and to complete the displays you need to address the problem.

Step 1: Geocode the data

Geocoding is the process of assigning a geographic location to an address. The accuracy of geocoding depends upon the accuracy of both the addresses you have and the reference street data used to find the geographic location.

A. Geocode police stations

1. Add the following feature classes from **OurWorld4\Module3\Project1\data**:

    - *aug06.xls (Double-click aug06.xls and add click_here_for_August_Crim$)*
    - *police_stations*
    - *usa_sts (in Houston.gdb)*

2. Open ArcToolbox and expand Geocoding Tools.

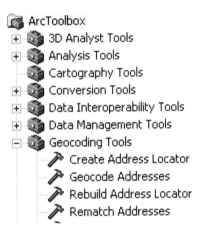

3. Double-click Create Address Locator.

4. For the Address Locator Style, select "US Streets."

5. For the Reference Data, select usa_sts and under Role select Primary table.

6. Store the Address Locator in the Project1_results.gdb and name it **Houston**.

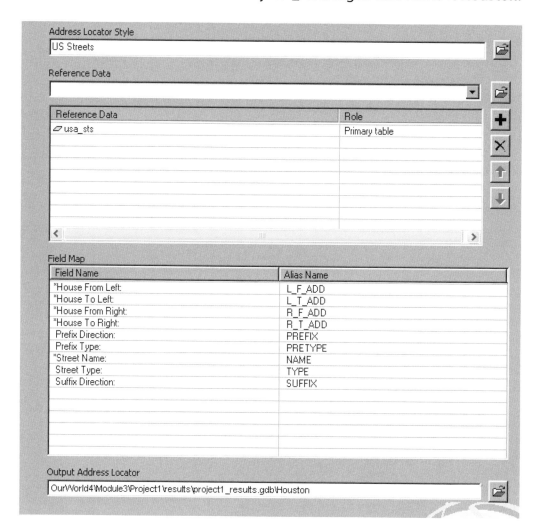

7. Click OK.

8. Right-click police_stations and select Geocode Addresses. The Houston Address Locator is already entered.

9. Click OK. You have the option of saving the file as a shapefile or a geodatabase feature class. Store the file as a feature class inside the Project1_results.gdb.

10. Name the file **police_stations**.

11. Click Save and OK.

Q6 *Were there any unmatched addresses?*

12. Click Done.

13. Remove police_stations.txt.

B. Geocode crime

1. Right-click the Crim$sheet and select Geocode Addresses. The Houston address locator is already entered.

2. Click OK.

3. In the Geocode Addresses menu, click Geocoding Options. Set the Spelling sensitivity to 60 and the Minimum match score to 40.

4. Click OK.

5. The Street or Intersection should be set to Street Name.

6. Name the file **geocoded_crime**.

7. Click OK.

Q7 *How many of the addresses were unmatched?*

Q8 *How many total crimes were there?*

Q9 *What percentage of the crimes was unmatched?*

8. You need to keep only the crimes with addresses that were matched in your file. Go to Selection by Attribute and choose Score>0.

9. Right-click Geocoding Results and select Data/Export. Click OK. Export the file as a geodatabase feature class and call it **raw_crime**. Click Save. Click OK.

10. Remove the Geocoding Result: geocoded_crime.

11. Remove click_here_for_August_2006.

12. Save the map document.

Step 2: Produce a basemap of Houston

1. Symbolize the police stations. (For this exercise you should use the More Symbols option in the Symbol Selector window and add the symbols for "Crime Analysis.")

2. Import the usa_sts.lyr layer. Accept CLASS_RTE as the Value Field. Click OK. Click OK.

3. Check the raw_crime data and make sure all the crimes are from August 2006. If you open the attribute table for raw_crime and sort in ascending order by Offense_Date, you will see records that are not from the month of August 2006. Select all the files that are not from August 2006.

(Q10) *How many records are not from August 2006?*

With those records selected, click Options and select Switch Selection.

4. Export this selection and save the feature class as **crime** to eliminate the extraneous records. Remove raw_crime.

5. Open the attribute table for crime and carefully study the data.

(Q11) *How many crime records are listed?*

(Q12) *Can multiple records (crime incidents) occur at the same location? Give an example.*

(Q13) *Can you suggest a reason for this?*

(Q14) *How is the Offense_Time represented?*

(Q15) *What are the offenses recorded?*

For additional information about Texas Criminal Codes, go to http://www.sadwilawyer.com/ texas%20law.htm.

6. Open the attribute table for crime, right-click Offense and select Summarize to summarize the crimes.

7. Name the summary file **total_crime** as a dBASE table and save it in your results folder geodatabase. Add the file to the table of contents.

8. Open the total_crime attribute table. Turn on the Editor Toolbar and start editing total_crime in the **/results/project1_results.gdb** folder. Change the offense labels as follows:

Original Name	New Name
Aggravated Assault	Assault
Auto Theft	Auto Theft
Burglary	Burglary
Burglary of a Motor Vehicle	Burglary/Auto
Narcotic Drug Laws	Drugs
Driving While Intoxicated	DWI
Murder & Nonnegligent Manslaughter	Murder
Forcible Rape	Rape
Robbery	Robbery

9. Stop editing and save.

10. From the Tools menu, select Graphs/Create to open the Create Graph Wizard.

11. For Graph Type select Vertical Bar.

12. For Layer/Table select Total_crime.

13. For Value Field select Count_Offense.

14. For X field select Count_Offense and Ascending.

15. For the X label field select Offense.

16. For Color select Palette and Excel.

17. Select Next.

18. Check Graph in 3D view.

19. For title enter **Total Crime in Houston, August 2006**.

20. Click Finish.

21. Right-click the blue bar at the top and Select Add to Layout.

22. Save the map document as **crime1**.

▶ Deliverable 1: A basemap of Houston showing police stations, crimes, roads and census blocks. Include a graph of total crimes.

Step 3: Produce a map of police stations with crime proximity

There are a number of ways to explore the spatial prevalence of crime in Houston. You'll use two different methods to calculate the proximity of crime to the police stations. First, you'll create buffers of fixed distance to see how many crimes occur within 2, 4, or 6 miles of the police stations. Then, you'll use the technique of a spatial join to connect each crime to the nearest police station.

1. Open a new map document and save it as **crime2**.

2. Add Houston.

3. Refer back to "Organize and document your work" and do the following:

   a. *Document the map.*

   b. *Set the data frame properties. They must be set for each data frame.*

   c. *Set the environments.*

4. Add police_stations, highways, and crime. Symbolize the feature classes appropriately.

To allocate personnel and project where to build new substations, the police need to know where personnel resources are strained.

5. Open ArcToolbox, expand Analysis Tools, and expand Proximity. Double-click Multiple Ring Buffer.

6. The Input feature is police_stations. Name the output feature class **buffer**.

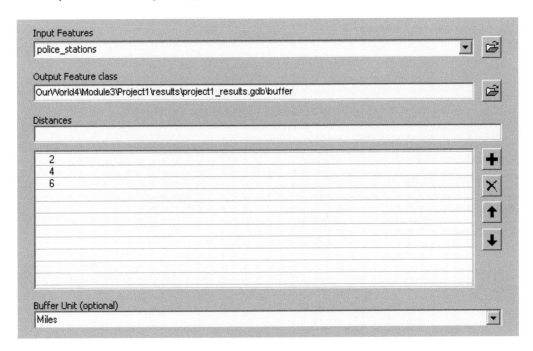

7. Set the buffer unit to be miles and the distances to be 2, 4, and 6.

Now that there are buffer zones around the police stations, perform a spatial join with crime. A spatial join appends one feature class's attribute table to another based on the relative locations of the features in the two layers. To do a spatial join, you need each crime to count as one event.

8. Open the attribute table of crime and add a short integer field and call it **Event**.

9. Use the Field Calculator to perform the following operation: Event = 1. Close the attribute table.

10. Right-click buffer, click Joins and Relates and select Join to connect each crime to the appropriate buffer. In the drop-down menu beneath "What do you want to join to this layer?" choose "Join data from another layer based on spatial location," and then choose the crime layer. This will spatially join the crimes to the appropriate buffer so that you'll know how many crimes occur within the specified miles of each police station.

11. Name the file **buf_crime**. Click OK. Display buf_crime by unique value with distance as the Value field.

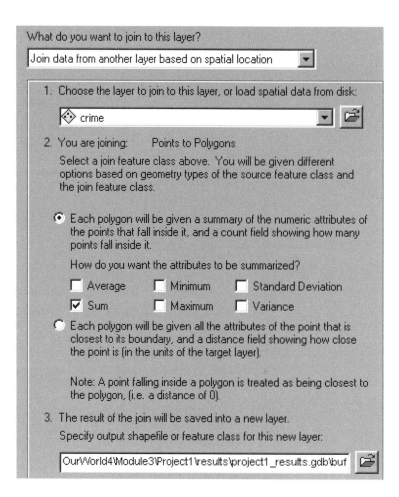

12. Remove buffer from the table of contents.

Q16 *Complete this table on your worksheet: (Hint: Use the Sum_event field.)*

Remember, there are 6,834 crimes.

Distance In Miles	Crimes	Percent
2		
4		
6		
More than 6		

Q17 *What do these results tell the police department about the distribution of crime?*

The table above shows one method to categorize the crime by location using distance buffers. Another way to characterize the crime distribution is to do a spatial join of all the crimes with the nearest police station. When you spatially join crimes to police stations, ArcGIS gives a summary of the numeric attributes of the features in the layer being joined (crimes) that are CLOSEST to each feature in the base layer (police_stations) and a count field showing how many crimes are closest to each station.

13. Right-click police_stations and select Joins and Relates. Again choose "Join Data from Another Layer Based on Spatial Location." The layer to join is Crime.

14. Name the output layer **pol_sta_crimes**. Click OK.

Q18 *Use the attribute table of pol_sta_crimes to complete this table on your worksheet:*

Remember, there are 6,834 crimes.

Police Station	Number Of Crimes	Percent
Central		
Clear Lake		
East (Magnolia)		
Fondren		
HPD Headquarters		
Intercontinental Airport		
Kingwood		
North		
Northeast		
Northwest		
South Central		
Southeast		
Southwest		
Westside		

15. Display the number of crimes for each station as a bar chart using sum_event as the value field.

Q19 *What does this method tell the police department about the distribution of crime?*

Q20 *Compare the two methods of analysis.*

Q21 *Write a spatial analysis of crimes and police stations.*

16. Save your map document as **crime2**.

▶ Deliverable 2: A map of police stations and locations of crimes along with recommendations for new police substations sites.

Step 4: Produce density maps of auto theft, burglary, and narcotics-related crimes

You will use the ArcGIS Spatial Analyst extension for the next part of the project. The Spatial Analyst tools allow you to calculate a continuous distribution of a particular type of crime from a set of input points. This density "surface" provides data throughout your area of interest and gives you a better indication of the distribution of crime in that area. Density maps are frequently used in crime analysis to show where crimes are concentrated and to aid the search for patterns.

1. Open a new map document and save it as **crime3**.

2. Turn on the Spatial Analyst extension.

3. Add Houston.

4. Refer to "Organizing and documenting your work" and do the following:

   a. Document the map.
   b. Set the data frame properties. They must be set for each data frame.
   c. Set the environments.

5. Add crime.

To calculate a density map, the computer needs to have a numerical value for each event (text fields won't work). Remember that you added an Event field and a 1 for each crime in step 3 above.

You are now ready to create a density map. The police department is particularly interested in aggravated assault, burglary, and narcotics-related crime.

6. Select all the burglaries. Do not include "Burglary of a Motor Vehicle."

Q22 *How many burglaries have been reported?*

7. Open ArcToolbox, expand Spatial Analyst Tools, expand Density, and double-click Kernel Density.

8. The input feature is Crime and the population field is Event.

9. The output raster should be named **burglary** and the search radius set to 5,000.

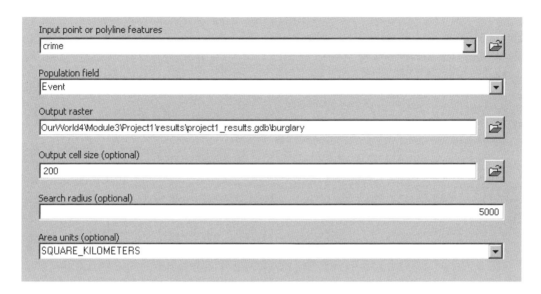

10. Click OK.

11. Clear the selected features in crime and turn crime off.

12. Move the density map above Houston so you can see the results.

Density maps can be hard to interpret in the initial symbology. Statistically, the map says that in the darkest blue area there are 1.5 burglaries per square kilometer. It is easier to interpret the map if you classify the crime density using natural breaks.

13. For this burglary density map and the other density maps, classify the data using natural breaks with five classes labeled as follows:

    1. *Low*

    2. *Low Medium*

    3. *Medium*

    4. *High Medium*

    5. *High*

14. Save the Layer File as **crime**. A layer file cannot be stored in a geodatabase. Put the layer file in the results folder.

15. Add main_usa_sts and symbolize.

Q23 *What is the spatial distribution of burglaries in Houston?*

16. Name the data frame **burglary**.

17. Insert another data frame and name it **narcotics**.

Remember to set the coordinate system for the data frame properties. Repeat above procedure for narcotics-related crimes. Import the crime layer file to use the same symbology for these crimes.

Q24 *What is the spatial distribution of drug crimes in Houston?*

18. Repeat the above procedure for aggravated assault.

Q25 *Describe the spatial distribution of aggravated assault crimes in the Houston area.*

19. Produce a presentation map showing aggravated assault, burglary, and narcotics-related crimes.

20. Add the census block groups (blkgrp) to each of the crime data frames.

21. Display the census block by quantities using population density (POP00_SQMI) as the value field.

22. Move the crime density maps above the population density maps.

23. Turn on the Effects Toolbar and use the Swipe tool to compare the crime density map with the population density. The Swipe tool allows you to reveal what's underneath a particular layer. Make sure the top layer is shown in the Effects Toolbar.

24. Save the map document.

▶ **Deliverable 3: Density maps of aggravated assault, burglary, and narcotics-related crimes.**

Step 5: Produce time crime maps

1. Open a new map document and save it as **crime4**.

2. Add Houston.

3. Refer back to "Organizing and documenting your work" and do the following:

   a. *Document the map.*

   b. *Set the data frame properties. They must be set for each data frame.*

   c. *Set the environments.*

4. Add crime.

When you open the crime attribute table you will find that Offense_Ti (time) is given on a 24-hour clock. The table below helps you convert time to a 12-hour clock.

12-hour Clock	24-hour Clock
12:00 midnight	0000 hrs
1:00 AM	0100 hrs
2:00 AM	0200 hrs
3:00 AM	0300 hrs
4:00 AM	0400 hrs
5:00 AM	0500 hrs
6:00 AM	0600 hrs
7:00 AM	0700 hrs
8:00 AM	0800 hrs
9:00 AM	0900 hrs
10:00 AM	1000 hrs
11:00 AM	1100 hrs
12:00 noon	1200 hrs
1:00 PM	1300 hrs
2:00 PM	1400 hrs
3:00 PM	1500 hrs
4:00 PM	1600 hrs
5:00 PM	1700 hrs
6:00 PM	1800 hrs
7:00 PM	1900 hrs
8:00 PM	2000 hrs
9:00 PM	2100 hrs
10:00 PM	2200 hrs
11:00 PM	2300 hrs
12:00 midnight	2400 hrs

5. Open the attribute table and study the Offense_Ti field. Sort the records in ascending order for Offense_Ti.

This analysis will be easier if the time is expressed in hours and not hours and minutes. If you could truncate the last two digits, you would have just the hour in which the crime occurred.

6. Add a short integer field called **Hours**.

7. Right-click Hours and open the Field Calculator. Enter the following expression in the box in the Field Calculator window to retain only the first two digits of the time: **Left([Offense_Ti],2)**

8. Click OK.

9. Sort the Hours field in ascending order. It now starts at midnight, and the last hour is 23.

Q26 *What is the total number of crimes?*

Q27 *Calculate crime for various time periods by completing this table on your worksheet:*

Time	Name	24-Hour Clock	Crimes	Percent
midnight–6:00 AM	night	00–06		
6:00 AM–noon	morning	06–12		
noon–6:00 PM	afternoon	12–18		
6:00 PM–midnight	evening	18–24		

Hours >= 0 AND Hours < 6   Night
Hours >= 6 AND Hours < 12   Morning
Hours >= 12 AND Hours < 18   Afternoon
Hours >= 18 AND Hours <=23   Evening

10. Graphically represent crime for a 24-hour period.

     a. *Clear Selected Features.*

     b. *Right-click the field heading Hours and select Summarize.*

     c. *Name the file* **totalcrime_hrs**. *Save as a File Geodatabase table. Click OK.*

     d. *Check Yes to add the result table in the map.*

     e. *Go to Tools/Graph and open the Create Graph Wizard.*

    i.   Select a Vertical Bar for the Graph Type.

    ii.   Select Totalcrime_hrs for the Layer/Table.

    iii.   For the Value Field select Count_hours.

    iv.   Label the x field by Hours.

11. Save the map document as **crime4**.

Q28 *What time of day is crime the lowest?*

Q29 *What time of day is crime the highest?*

12. Create a series of auto theft density maps. Using the procedure in step 3, produce auto theft density maps for six-hour periods (midnight–6:00 AM, 6:00 AM–noon, noon–6:00 PM, 6:00 PM–midnight). Save each density map and name the files **night, morning, afternoon,** and **evening**, respectively. Use the multiple variable selection shown in the table on page 88. Hint: Select Auto Theft and use the "AND" operator to select the appropriate time. For example: "Offense"='Auto Theft' AND "Hours">=6 AND "Hours"<12.

13. Create maps using Kernel Density with Event as the Population field. Pick the density map that has the highest auto theft (.901) and use that file to define the symbology. Classify using Equal Interval and 5 Classes. Format the labels to have only 2 decimals. Save this as a layer file and name it **auto_theft**.

14. Import this layer file into each of the other auto theft density layers to use the same symbology for each layer.

15. Remove crime.

16. Save the map document as **crime4**.

▶ Deliverable 4: A graph exploring the time of day crimes are committed.

Once your analysis is complete, you're not done. You still need to develop a solution to the original problem and present your results in a compelling way to your audience for the particular situation. The presentation of your various data displays must explain what they show and how they contribute to solving the problem.

Module 3: Project 1

Presentation

Write a report documenting your analysis and addressing the needs of the Houston Police Department. Remember that the members of the Houston Police Department probably lack your in-depth knowledge of GIS, so you'll need to communicate your results without technical jargon and explain the importance of the various deliverables. Make specific recommendations on where to build new substations and clearly show concentrations of different crimes.

Extending the project

Your instructor may choose for you to complete this optional exercise.

Evaluate drug-free zones

In the state of Texas there are drug-free zones within 1,000 feet of schools. Anyone arrested for dealing drugs within these zones faces extra-stiff mandatory penalties. To document the effectiveness of these laws, calculate the number of crimes within 1,000 feet of the schools in Houston.

Q30 *How many schools do not have any crime within the 1,000-foot zone?*

Q31 *What school has the highest number of crimes nearby?*

Q32 *Select that school and see which crimes were committed.*

Q33 *Is the drug-free zone effective?*

Q34 *How could you design a study to find out what is going on just outside the zone?*

M ● ● ● ○ ○
P ● ○ ○ ○

Module 3: Project 2 ●●○

Logging Lincoln's police activity

Scenario

In this exercise you have been hired as a consultant to the Lincoln, Nebraska, Police Department to help assess the allocation of police resources and the geographic distribution of crimes.

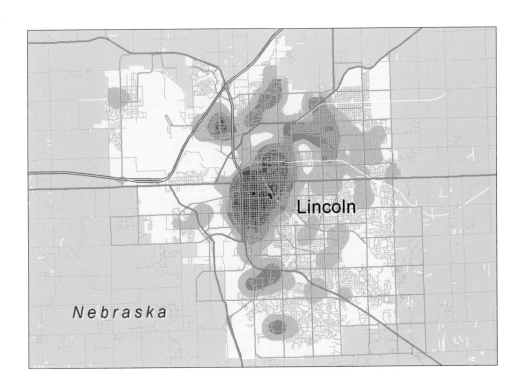

Problem

The Lincoln Police Department knows the value of using GIS for crime analysis and wants to investigate the following:

- Crime patterns in proximity to police stations to determine if current patrols are effective or adjustments are necessary, such as reorganizing beats and building new substations.
- Patterns of crime by days of the week.
- Patterns of assault, burglary, and shoplifting.
- Patterns of when crimes are committed.

Reminder

It helps to divide a large problem into a set of smaller tasks such as the following:

- Identify the geographic study area.
- Determine the sequence of steps in your study.
- Identify the decisions to be made.
- Develop the information required to make decisions.
- Identify stakeholders for this issue.

Deliverables

We recommend the following deliverables for this problem:

1. A basemap of the Lincoln area showing police stations, roads, and crimes in August 2006. Include a graph of total crimes by days of the week.

2. A map of police stations and locations of crimes along with a recommendation of where to build new substations.

3. Density maps of assault, burglary, and shoplifting.

4. A graph exploring crime throughout a 24-hour period.

Examine the data

The data for this project is stored in the **OurWorld4\Module3\Project2\data** folder.

Reminder

You can explore the metadata in ArcCatalog. The table on the following page helps you organize this information.

Q1 *Investigate the metadata and complete this table on your worksheet:*

Layer	Data Type	Publication Information: Who Created The Data?	Time Period Data Is Relevant	Spatial Horizontal Coordinate System	Attribute Values
aug_06	Vector	Lincoln Police Department	2006	N/A	
blkgrp					
lincoln			2003		Census Data
usa_streets		Tele Atlas North America, Inc., ESRI		Geographic	Street Data

Organize and document your work

Reminder

- Set up the proper directory structure.
- Create a process summary.
- Document the map.
- Set the environments:
    a. Set the Data Frame Properties Coordinate System to UTM 1983 Zone 14N.
    b. Set the Working Directory.
    c. Set the Scratch Directory.
    d. Set the Output Coordinate System to "Same as Display."
    e. Set the Extent to Same As Layer Blkgrp or Lincoln.
    f. Set the Output Cell Size to 200.
    g. Set the Mask to Blkgrp or Lincoln.

Analysis

An important first step in GIS analysis is to develop a basemap of your study area. Complete deliverable 1 and answer the questions below to orient yourself to the study area.

Module 3: Project 2

93

▶ **Deliverable 1: A basemap of the Lincoln area showing police stations, crimes, roads, and census blocks in August 2006. Include a graph of total crimes by days of the week.**

Reminder

Be sure to create an address locator before you geocode the police stations.

Q2 *Were all the police stations matched when they were geocoded?*

Q3 *How many crimes have the day of the week recorded? Not recorded?*

Q4 *What percent did not record the day of the week?*

Q5 *Looking at the graph of crime by days of the week, what day(s) would require more of a police presence?*

▶ **Deliverable 2: A map of police stations and locations of crimes along with a recommendation of where to build new police substations.**

Reminder

- Set the buffer unit to miles and the distances to 1, 2, and 3.
- Add a field named **Event** and enter a **1** for each crime.
- Spatially join the crimes to the police station.

Q6 *How many total crimes are there?*

Q7 *Complete this table on your worksheet:*

Distance In Miles	Crimes	Percent
1		
2		
3		
More than 3		

Q8 *What does this method tell the police department about the distribution of crime?*

Q9 *Complete this table on your worksheet:*

Police Station	Number Of Crimes	Percent
'F' Street Community Center		
Auld Recreation Center		
Bess Dobson Walt Library		
Bryan/LGH		
Headquarters		
Highlands		
LMEF Inc.		
LPD Center Team Station		
Northeast Team Station		
Team Station		
Union College		

Q10 *What does this method tell the police department about the distribution of crime?*

Q11 *Compare the two methods of analysis.*

Q12 *Write a spatial analysis of crimes and police stations.*

▶ **Deliverable 3: Density maps of assault, burglary, and shoplifting.**

Reminder

- Set the coordinate system for the each data frame.
- Use Event as the population field.
- Use a radius of 1,000.

Study the document UCR CODES in the documents folder. In the attribute table, TYPE_CODE represents the UCR CODES.

Q13 *What are the code numbers for assault?*

Q14 *What are the code numbers for burglary?*

Q15 *What are the code numbers for shoplifting?*

Q16 *How many assaults occurred?*

Q17 *How many burglaries?*

Q18 *How many instances of shoplifting?*

Reminder

Classify the data using natural breaks with five classes. For all three crimes, create a single standard layer file of Low, Low Medium, Medium, High Medium, and High.

Q19 *Describe the spatial distribution of assault in Lincoln.*

Q20 *Describe the spatial distribution of burglary in Lincoln.*

Q21 *Describe the spatial distribution of shoplifting in Lincoln.*

▶ **Deliverable 4: A graph exploring crime throughout a 24-hour period.**

Reminder

Use the Field Calculator to change the Zulu time to hours. Use the TIME_FROM for your Time field and be sure to select only the records that have recorded times. You must not select any record that is not a standard Zulu time. In this database there are records that do not have a recorded time. There also are records that have unk or UNK, and there are incorrect records of 7130, 8-12, and a.m. DO NOT USE THESE RECORDS. Make sure your selection contains only records with times 0000 to 2400. The easiest way to do this is to select all the files that have a recorded time and export them to a new data file.

Q22 *Complete this table on your worksheet:*

Time	Name	Zulu Time	Crimes	Percent
midnight–6 AM	night	00–06		
6 AM–noon	morning	06–12		
noon–6 PM	afternoon	12–18		
6 PM–midnight	evening	18–24		

M ● ● ● ○ ○
P ● ● ○

Q23 *What is the total number of crimes with times?*

Q24 *What time of day is crime the lowest?*

Q25 *What time of day is crime the highest?*

Reminder

- Hours >= 0 AND Hours < 6 (night)
- Hours >= 6 AND Hours < 12 (morning)
- Hours >= 12 AND Hours < 18 (afternoon)
- Hours >= 18 AND Hours <=23 (evening)

Presentation

Remember to keep in mind the interests and expertise of your audience as you prepare your presentation. Remember to develop a solution to the original problem and present your results in a compelling way.

Module 3: Project 3 ● ● ●

On your own

You've worked through a guided activity on the variation of crime in a large urban area and you've repeated the analysis with data from a smaller city. In this section, you will reinforce the skills you've developed by researching and analyzing a similar scenario entirely on your own. First you must identify your study area and acquire the data for your analysis. Links to three jurisdictions with crime data posted online are listed below. However, if there is another area that has significant interest for you such as one that is more local, download and work with that data. If you plan to do your local area, be sensitive to the fact that some of the reports contain individual names which should be removed before you present any results.

- Sacramento, California: **http://www.sacpd.org/databases.asp**
- Houston, Texas: **http://www.houstontx.gov/police/stats.htm**
- Fairfax County, Virginia: **http://www.fairfaxcounty.gov/police/police7.htm**

Refer to your process summary and the preceding module project if you need help. Here are some basic steps to help you organize your work:

Research

Research the problem and answer the following questions:

1. What is the area of study?
2. What data is available?

Obtain the data

Do you have access to baseline data? The ESRI Data and Maps Media Kit provides many of the layers of data that are needed for project work. Be sure to pay particular attention to the source of data and get the latest version.

Obtaining crime data can be challenging. Much of the data is summarized or displayed in PDF format. If you are interested in doing a local crime study, ask your local police department for help. Tell your police department that you are not interested in individual names or addresses. Data by block is generally more than sufficient for your analysis.

If you do not have access to ESRI Data and Maps Media Kit, you can obtain data from the following sources:

- http://www.esri.com/tiger
- http://www.geographynetwork.com
- http://www.nationalatlas.gov

Workflow

After researching the problem and obtaining the data, you should do the following:

1. Write a brief scenario.
2. State the problem.
3. Define the deliverables.
4. Examine the data using ArcCatalog.
5. Set the directory structure, start your process summary, and document the map.
6. Decide what you need for the data frame coordinate system and the environments.
   a. What is the best projection for your work?
   b. Do you need to set a cell size or mask?
7. Start your analysis.
8. Prepare your presentation and deliverables.

Always remember to document your work in a process summary.

MODULE 4

Hurricane damage decisions

Introduction

In 2005, Hurricanes Katrina, Rita, and Wilma destroyed homes, businesses, infrastructure, and natural resources along the Gulf and Atlantic coasts. In the aftermath of the storms, federal, state, and local governments, service agencies, and the private sector responded by helping to rebuild the hurricane-ravaged areas and restore the local economies. GIS helped responders assess damage, monitor the weather, coordinate relief efforts, and track health hazards, among many other critical tasks, by providing relevant and readily available data, maps, and images. In this module, you will access some of the same data that guided critical decisions, such as funding and safety measures, in the wake of Hurricanes Katrina and Wilma. You will map elevations and bathymetry, analyze flooded areas and storm surges, and pinpoint vulnerable infrastructure. In the real world, this process saves lives, time, and money.

Projects in this module:

- **Coastal flooding from Hurricane Katrina**

- **Hurricane Wilma storm surge**

- **On your own**

Module worksheets

The student worksheet files can be found on the Data and Resources DVD.

Project 1 student sheet

- File name: Katrina_student_worksheet.doc
- Location: OurWorld4\Module4\Project1\documents
- Document length: 6 pages
- Worksheet for "Coastal flooding from Hurricane Katrina." A form for answering questions, completing tables, and tracking work to be handed in.

Project 2 student sheet

- File name: Wilma_student_worksheet.doc
- Location: OurWorld4\Module4\Project2\documents
- Document length: 3 pages
- Worksheet for "Hurricane Wilma storm surge." A form for answering questions, completing tables, and tracking work to be handed in.

Module 4: Project 1 ●○○○

Coastal flooding from Hurricane Katrina

Scenario

On Monday, August 29, 2005, Hurricane Katrina hit the Gulf Coast of the United States, devastating the wetlands and barrier islands. Three counties in Mississippi were particularly hard hit. To assess and remediate the damage caused by the 15-foot storm surge that hit the coast, your team of GIS specialists must prepare maps and calculate damage. The information will help federal officials decide how to allocate redevelopment resources.

The Gulf Coast contains much of the nation's fragile coastal ecosystem. The barrier islands, coastal wetlands, and forest wetlands each play a critical role in the environment. The barrier islands prevent storm surge and saltwater intrusion. Coastal wetlands provide habitat for mammals and waterfowl while also serving as a nursery for the Gulf fishing industry. Forest wetlands provide a renewable resource for the paper and timber industry.

Problem

Federal officials need to decide where to allocate disaster aid to the Mississippi counties most affected by Hurricane Katrina. You will assess the total acreage of different types of land cover that were under water as a result of the Katrina storm surge. The damage reflects the unique hydrography of the Gulf Coast, so you must map that as well. You also will map damage to the infrastructure and health care centers so that restoration efforts can focus on areas with the greatest need. Your team must prioritize locations for disaster aid, justified by the data provided and the maps, graphs, and tables you produce. As with many of the complex problems that confront us, there is not a single "right" answer. However, some answers are better supported and justified than others.

In applying GIS to a problem, it is critical that you have a very clear understanding of the problem or scenario. We find it helpful to answer these four questions, which test your understanding and divide the problem into smaller problems that are easier to solve.

Q1 *What geographic area are you studying? (Record answers on your worksheet.)*

Q2 *What decision do you need to make?*

Q3 *What information would help you make the decision?*

Q4 *Who are the key stakeholders for this issue? (This step is important. You need to know the audience for your analysis to help decide how to present your results.)*

Deliverables

After identifying the problem you're trying to solve, you need to envision the kinds of data displays (maps, graphs, and tables) that will address the problem.

We recommend the following deliverables for this exercise:

1. A map showing elevation/bathymetry of the Mississippi Coast counties with places, types of water, barrier islands, and hydrography.
2. A map of flooded land of the Mississippi Coast after Hurricane Katrina.
3. A bar graph showing percentage of total flooded land by land-cover type.
4. A map showing infrastructure and health facilities at risk from storm surge.
5. A table showing various land types that were flooded measured in acres and square miles.

Examine the data

The next step in your workflow is to identify, collect, and examine the data. Here, we've identified and collected the data layers you will need. Explore the data to discover information the various layers contain. The land-cover layer is a feature class that has been derived and processed from satellite imagery to show the different kinds of land cover in this region.

You can use ArcCatalog to preview the GIS data and explore the metadata associated with each feature class.

1. Open ArcCatalog and connect to the folder **OurWorld4\Module4\Project1\ data.**

2. Expand the data folder in the Catalog tree and double-click the Katrina geodatabase.

3. Click the Preview tab, then preview the geography and table for each feature class in the geodatabase.

The spatial coordinate system, the resolution of the data, and the attributes are all important pieces of information about each feature class. You will need this information for your analysis. Fortunately, the metadata allows you to access this information. Note that metadata can often be incomplete.

Q5 *Investigate the metadata and complete this table on your worksheet:*

Layer	Data Type	Publication Information: Who Created The Data?	Time Period Data Is Relevant	Spatial Horizontal Coordinate System	Attribute Values	Resolution For Rasters
airports	Vector				N/A	N/A
churches					N/A	N/A
counties			2001			N/A
elev				Geographic: GCS_North_ American_1983	Elevation is expressed in meters	1 arc second 0.000278 decimal degrees 30 meters
hospitals	Vector			Geographic	N/A	N/A
landcover	Vaster		2001			

107

In some cases, the values of the attributes can be difficult to understand without supplementary information. This is particularly true for the land-cover raster. The U.S. Geological Survey National Land Cover Class definitions are given in **OurWorld4\Module4\Project1\documents** folder in the Microsoft Excel file **NLCD_classification.xls.**

4. Close ArcCatalog.

Now that you've explored the available data, you're almost ready to begin your analysis. First you need to start a process summary, document your project, and set the project environments.

Organize and document your work

Step 1: Examine the directory structure

The next phase in a GIS project is to carefully keep track of the data and your calculations. You will work with a number of different files and it is important to keep them organized so you can easily find them. The best way to do this is to have a folder for your project that contains a data folder. For this project, the folder called **OurWorld4\Module4\Project1** will be your project folder. Make sure that it is stored in a place where you have write access. You can store your data inside the results folder. The results folder already contains an empty geodatabase named **project1_results**. Save your map documents inside the **OurWorld4\Module4\Project1\results** folder.

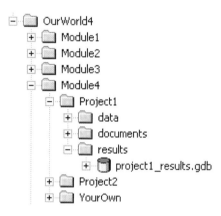

Step 2: Create a process summary

The process summary is just a list of the steps you used to do your analysis. We suggest a simple text document for your process summary. Keep adding to it as you do your work to avoid forgetting any steps. The list below shows an example of the first few entries in a process summary:

1. Explore the data.
2. Produce a map with elevation and bathymetry, counties, places, and islands.
3. Change elevation from meters to feet.
4. Isolate the flooded land.

Step 3: Document the map

You need to add descriptive properties to every map document you produce. You may use the same descriptive properties listed below for every map document in the module or individualize the documentation from map to map.

1. Open ArcMap and save a new map document as **coast1**.

2. From the File menu, choose Document Properties and in the dialog box add a title, author, and some descriptive text.

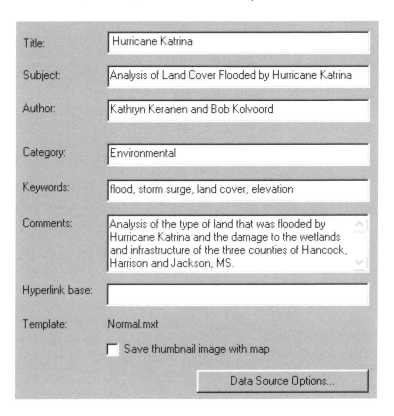

3. Click Data Source Options and then click the radio button to store relative paths of data sources. Click OK in both dialog boxes.

Storing relative paths allows ArcMap to automatically find all relevant data if you move your project folder to a new location or computer.

Step 4: Set the environments

In GIS analysis, you will often get data from various sources and this data may be in different coordinate systems and/or map projections. When using GIS to perform area calculations, you would like your result to be in familiar units, such as miles or kilometers. Data in an unprojected geographic coordinate system has units of decimal degrees, which are difficult to interpret. Thus, your calculations will be more meaningful if all the feature classes involved are in the same map projection. Fortunately, ArcMap can do much of this work for you if you set certain environment variables and data frame properties. In this step, you'll learn how to change these settings.

To display your data correctly, you'll need to set the coordinate system for the data frame. When you add data with a defined coordinate system, ArcMap will automatically set the data frame's projection to match the data. If you add subsequent layers that have a coordinate system different from the data frame, they are automatically projected on-the-fly to the data frame's coordinate system.

1. From the View menu, choose Data Frame Properties. Click the Coordinate System tab. Click Import. Navigate to your data folder, select landcover from the Katrina geodatabase, and click Add. Click OK.

Before using ArcToolbox tools to make your calculations, you should establish some general environment settings that apply to all of the tools you'll be using. The analysis environment includes the workspace where results will be placed, and the extent, cell size, and coordinate system for the results.

2. Open ArcToolbox, right-click any empty space within ArcToolbox, and choose Environments.

3. Expand General Settings.

By default, inputs and outputs are placed in your current workspace, but you can redirect the output to another workspace such as your results folder.

4. Set the Current Workspace as **OurWorld4\Module4\Data\Project1\data\Katrina.gdb**.

5. Set the Scratch Workspace as **OurWorld4\Module4\Project1\results\project1_results.gdb**.

6. For Output Coordinate System, select "Same as Display."

7. Expand Raster Analysis Settings.

8. Set the Cell size to 30.

You also want to limit your analysis to the three Mississippi Coast counties most affected by the storm. This is accomplished by using an analysis mask. The mask identifies those locations within the analysis extent that will be included when using a tool.

9. Set the Mask to Counties from the Katrina geodatabase.

10. Click OK.

Analysis

Once you've examined the data, completed map documentation, and set the environments, you are ready to begin the analysis and to prepare the displays to address the flooding problem. A good place to start any GIS analysis is to produce a locational or basemap to better understand the distribution of features in the geographic area you're studying. First, you will prepare a basemap of the Mississippi Coast showing the elevation of land and ocean floor.

Step 1: Display the Mississippi Coast's elevation, bathymetry, and hydrography

1. Add the Elevation raster (elev) to the map document. The elevation feature class shows elevation above sea level for land and bathymetry for the ocean floor.

2. Examine the elev feature class.

3. Open the layer properties for elev. Click the Symbology tab.

Q6 *What are the highest and lowest elevations?*

4. Symbolize elev with the Yellow to Green to Dark Blue color ramp. Check the box to invert the color ramp.

5. Collapse the legend.

6. Add counties and make them hollow.

7. Open the layer properties for counties. Click the Labels tab. Change the Label Field from STATE to COUNTY.

8. Click OK.

9. Right-click counties and Label Features.

Q7 *What are the names of the counties in order from west to east?*

10. Add places. Choose an appropriate symbology.

11. Add islands and label them.

12. Add water and symbolize it with Unique Values using the FTYPE field. Make the Swamp/Marsh type a distinct color or symbol.

13. Add rivers and make them an appropriate color.

14. Save the map document as **coast1**.

▶ Deliverable 1: A layout view map showing elevation, hydrography, and bathymetry of the Mississippi Coast counties with places, types of water, barrier islands, and hydrography.

Q8 *What does this map show you about the Gulf Coast?*

Q9 *Describe the spatial distribution of features.*

Q10 *How might these be affected by a large storm surge?*

Module 4: Project 1

111

With your first deliverable complete, you are ready to begin the quantitative analysis of the problem. Steps 2-5 will lead you through the identification of the land most affected by the storm surge and its land-cover type.

Step 2: Calculate flooded land

1. Open a new map document and save it as **coast2**.

2. Refer back to "Organize and document your work" and do the following:

   a. *Document the map.*

   b. *Set the data frame properties. They must be set for each data frame.*

   c. *Set the environments.*

3. Turn on the Spatial Analyst extension.

4. Add elev.

The elevation data is given in meters. The storm surge was given as 15 feet. To convert elev from meters to feet, multiply each elevation in elev by 3.28 because there are 3.28 feet in a meter.

5. In ArcToolbox, expand the Spatial Analyst Tools toolbox and then expand the Math toolset.

6. Open the Times tool. For input raster or constant value 1, choose elev. For input raster or constant value 2, enter **3.28**. Save the output raster as **elev_ft** in your Project1_results geodatabase. Click OK. The new raster is added to the table of contents.

7. Remove elev from the table of contents.

8. The next step is to isolate the area flooded by the storm surge. Expand the Logical toolset in the Math menu and use the Less than Equal tool to select elev_ft less than or equal to 15.

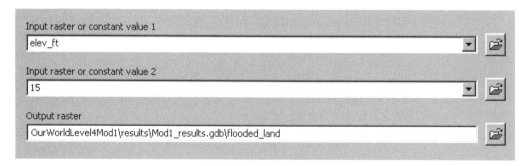

9. Save the output raster as **flooded_land** in your project1_results geodatabase.

10. Remove elev_ft from the table of contents.

11. Save your map document.

Anything that has a value of 1 fits the established flood criteria of less than or equal to 15 feet. Thus the value of 1 represents the flooded land.

Now that you've identified which land is flooded, you need to determine the type of land cover for the flooded land.

Step 3: Reclassify national land cover

The 16 separate land-cover classification categories in the land-cover raster are too specific for your purposes, so you will group similar classifications to reduce the number of categories to six, which represents distinctly different kinds of land cover, as shown in the table below.

1. Add landcover.

2. Open the landcover Properties dialog box and symbolize by Unique Values. Click OK.

3. In ArcToolbox, expand the Spatial Analysis Tools and then expand the Reclass toolset, and open the Reclassify tool. For input raster, choose land-cover. For Reclass field, choose VALUE. Click Unique. For each old value, type the value from the table below in the New Values column.

Original Values	Type Of Land	Reclassified Values	Type Of Land
11	Open Water	1	Water
21	Developed, Open Space	2	Developed
22	Developed, Low Intensity	2	
23	Developed, Medium Intensity	2	
24	Developed, High Intensity	2	
31	Barren Land	3	Barren
41	Deciduous Forest	4	Forest
42	Evergreen Forest	4	
43	Mixed Forest	4	
52	Scrub/Shrub	5	Agriculture
71	Grassland/Herbaceous	5	
81	Pasture/Hay	5	
82	Cultivated Crops	5	
90	Woody Wetlands	6	Wetlands
95	Emergent Herbaceous Wetland	6	
127	No Data	0	No Data

113

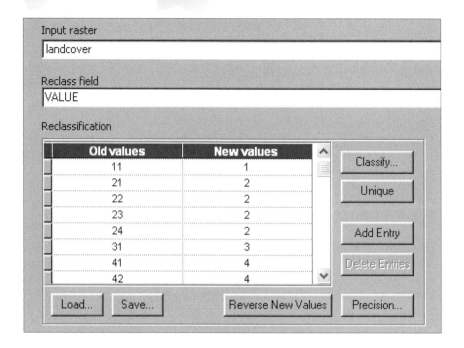

4. Save the output raster as **reclandcover** in your project1_results geodatabase.

5. Click OK.

6. Remove landcover.

7. Save your map document.

Step 4: Isolate the flooded land cover

To calculate the flooded land areas and classify it by land cover, you need to isolate the flooded areas. To do this, you must multiply the flooded_land by reclandcover.

1. Use the Times tool to multiply flooded_land by reclandcover.

2. Save the output raster as **floodedlc** in your project1_results geodatabase.

3. Click OK.

4. Remove reclandcover and flooded_land from the table of contents.

5. Save your map document.

Step 5: Label the reclassified flooded land cover

1. Open the floodedlc attribute table and click Options and select Add Field.

2. Name the new field TYPE and make it a text field with a length of 20.

3. Turn on the Editor toolbar. From the Editor menu, select Start Editing. If asked, make sure to select the results folder as the location from which to edit.

4. Enter the correct land cover for each type of land. Label the land as follows:

   0 = Not Flooded

   1 = Water

   2 = Barren

   3 = Developed

   4 = Forest

   5 = Agriculture

   6 = Wetlands

5. In the Editor toolbar, select Save Edits and Stop Editing. Close the table.

6. Display by Unique Values with the Value Field TYPE and pick an appropriate color. Choose No Color for the Value of 0. That land is not flooded.

7. After labeling and selecting an appropriate color, click Apply and close the Properties dialog window.

8. Right-click floodedlc and select Save as a layer file in order to save the symbology you've just created.

9. Add counties and make them hollow. Label the counties. Remember to choose Label Features in Properties and select COUNTY as the Label field.

10. Add places and symbolize them appropriately.

11. Add islands, make them hollow, and label them.

12. Save the map document.

Q11 *Now that you have created the first part of deliverable 2, identify the extent of the flood damage, assess which areas were most affected, and summarize the damage to the counties and the barrier islands.*

The qualitative analysis above is a good start, but to make decisions about dealing with the damage from Hurricane Katrina requires a quantitative assessment of the acreage of each land type affected by the flood surge.

Step 6: Determine percentage of flooded land type

In this step, you will create a graph that shows the percentage of each type of land that was flooded. The developed and residential land will cost the most to rebuild now, but the wetland destruction may have a more lasting effect on the recovery of the economy and the environment.

To determine percentages, you will use the count field in the attribute table of floodedlc. This field tells you the number of pixels of each land type and you'll use that to measure area. You do not want to include land that was not flooded.

1. Open the floodedlc attribute table.

2. Select all types of land except Not Flooded.

3. Right-click Count and select Statistics.

Q12 *Record the sum, which represents the number of pixels that was flooded.*

4. Close the Statistics window.

5. In the Attributes table, Go to Options and add a field called **Percent.** The field type should be float.

6. Click OK.

7. Right-click the Percent field and select Field Calculator. Perform the following calculation:

   *COUNT/1380797 * 100*

Ignore the warning about calculating outside the editing session. It is always a good idea to verify that your percentages add up to 100.

8. Click Ok.

9. Close the attribute table.

Step 7: Graph the percentage of flooded land by land-cover type

1. In the Tools menu, select Graphs and click Create. The Create Graph Wizard will open. Select Vertical Bar as the Graph type.

2. Set the Layer/Table to be floodedlc.

3. For Value Field, select Percent.

4. For x field (optional) select Percent and Ascending.

5. For x Label Field, select Type.

6. Click Next.

7. Click the radio button that says, "Show only selected features/records on the graph."

8. Enter the title **Percentage of Flooded Land.**

9. Click Graph in 3D view. Click Finish.

10. Right-click the blue bar at the top of the graph and choose Add to layout.

11. For both the floodedlc map and the graph to appear on the layout you need to add floodedlc again and turn off the bottom floodedlc, but do not unselect the rows.

12. Create an appropriate layout.

13. Save the map document as **coast2**.

Deliverables 2 and 3 can be combined on the map layout or created separately.

▶ **Deliverable 2: A map of flooded land of the Mississippi Coast after Hurricane Katrina.**

▶ **Deliverable 3: A bar graph showing percentage of total flooded land by land-cover type.**

Q13 *What does the graph tell you about the greatest impact of the storm surge?*

Q14 *Describe the distribution of the flooded areas and how the flood might affect the long-term sustainability of the region.*

The storm surge affected more than just the wetlands. There are a variety of infrastructure elements that affect a region's economy and people's well-being. In this next step, you will explore the spatial distribution of the infrastructure in this region.

Step 8: Prepare a map showing infrastructure and health facility destruction

As in any disaster, health facilities and the infrastructure that enables people to access them are critical to evacuation and recovery.

1. Open a new map document and save it as **coast3.mxd**.

2. Refer back to "Organize and document your work" and do the following:

    a. *Document the map.*

    b. *Set the data frame properties. They must be set for each data frame.*

    c. *Set the environments.*

3. Add counties.

4. Add usa_streets. Open the layer properties symbology.

5. Go to Symbology and import the Streets.lyr file. In the Import Symbology Matching dialog box that appears, click OK.

6. Label the major interstate and U.S. highways.

7. Add railroads and symbolize appropriately.

8. Add hospitals and symbolize appropriately.

9. Add churches and symbolize appropriately

10. Add flooded_land. Make the 0 values have No Color and pick a color for the 1 values and make it 25% transparent by selecting the Display tab in the Properties window and entering **25** in the Transparency box.

11. Save the map document as **coast3**.

▶ Deliverable 4: A map showing infrastructure and health facilities at risk from the storm surge.

Q15 *Describe the distribution of infrastructure and health facilities and which elements have likely been damaged in the storm surge.*

Q16 *How might you prioritize the damaged elements that should be restored first?*

Step 9: Calculate acreage

The final step in your analysis is to calculate the acreage of the flooded areas. This information will allow your team, other government agencies, and insurance firms to make damage assessments.

When you set the data frame coordinate system to that of the landcover raster (Albers conic equal area), all of the cells have a spatial unit of meters.

1. Open a new map document and save it as **coast4.mxd**.

2. Refer back to "Organize and document your work" and do the following:

    a. *Document the map.*

    b. *Set the data frame properties. They must be set for each data frame.*

    c. *Set the environments.*

3. Add counties.

4. Add floodedlc.

These are the facts that you know:

- Each cell is 30 x 30 meters.
- There are 4,046.68 square meters in an acre.
- There are 640 acres in a square mile.

Q17 *If you add a field called ACRES and use the Field Calculator, write the formula that you would use to calculate acres.*

Q18 *If you add a field called SQMILES, write the formula that you would use to calculate square miles.*

5. Open the attribute table of floodedlc and add a float field named **ACRES**.

6. Use the field calculator to perform the following calculation:

   ACRES = COUNT*900/4046.68

7. Add a float field called **SQMILES**.

8. Use the field calculator to perform the following calculation:

   SQMILES = ACRES/640

9. From your earlier analysis, the land-cover types are in the following order (least to most area):

   - *Barren*
   - *Water*
   - *Agriculture*
   - *Forest*
   - *Developed*
   - *Wetlands*

Q19 *Complete this table on your worksheet:.*

Type Of Land	Acres	Square Miles

10. Save the project showing acreage as **coast4**.

▶ **Deliverable 5: A table showing various land types that were flooded measured in acres and square miles.**

Once your analysis is complete, you're not done. You still need to develop a solution to the original problem and present your results in a compelling way to the federal officials in this particular situation. The presentation of your various data displays must explain what they show and how they contribute to solving the problem.

Presentation

Write a report documenting your analysis and addressing how to allocate redevelopment funds to human, infrastructure, or natural resources. You must explain the spatial patterns you see and describe the implications of your calculations and analysis for this problem. Remember that your audience probably lacks your in-depth knowledge of GIS, so you'll need to communicate your results without using technical jargon and explain the importance of the various deliverables. Make specific recommendations as to which counties should get what amount of money and for what purpose.

Extending the project

Your instructor may have you complete these optional exercises.

Add layers to ArcGlobe

Use the 3D Analyst extension and open ArcGlobe. Add counties, floodedlc, and other appropriate layers to ArcGlobe. Zoom to the study area.

Q20 *What can you tell about the bathymetry of the area?*

Q21 *How would that affect the region's industries?*

Analyze flooded areas by county

Hurricane Katrina landed on the western side of Mississippi. Because of this western landing, the storm surge was actually greatest in Hancock and the least in Jackson. Do an individual county analysis. For Hancock, assume the maximum storm surge of 15 feet. For Harrison, assume a storm surge of 11 feet. For Jackson, assume a storm surge of 8 feet.

Module 4: Project 2 ●●○

Hurricane Wilma storm surge

Scenario

After stalling for several days over Cancun, Mexico, Hurricane Wilma approached the Florida Keys and strengthened to a category 3 storm before making landfall on October 19, 2005, at Key West, Florida. The greatest devastation caused by Wilma was not from the wind but from the storm surge, which was approximately eight feet. Sixty percent of the homes in Key West were flooded and tens of thousands of cars were submerged.

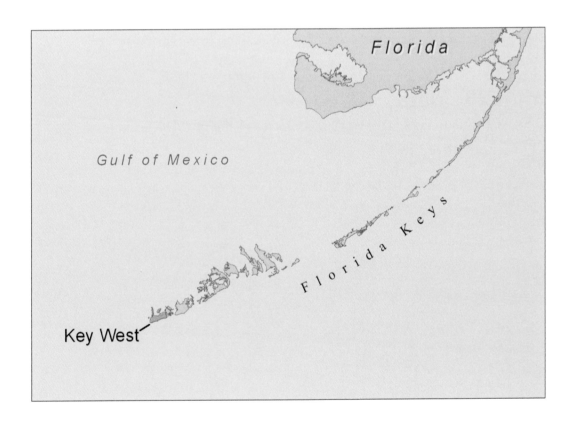

Problem

Most of Wilma's damage was caused by the surge on the morning after the storm. To settle thousands of claims, insurance companies needed maps showing the height of the surge. You are assigned to create maps to assess the total acreage of the different types of land cover that were under water as a result of the Wilma storm surge. You also must map damage to the infrastructure and health care centers so that restoration efforts can focus on the areas with the greatest need.

Reminder

It helps to divide a large problem such as this into a set of smaller tasks such as the following:

1. Identify the geographic study area.
2. Determine the sequence of steps in your study.
3. Identify the decisions to be made.
4. Develop the information required to make decisions.
5. Identify stakeholders for this issue.

Deliverables

We recommend the following deliverables for this problem:

1. A map of elevation and bathymetry of Key West with Key West places and streets.
2. A map of flooded land in Key West after the Wilma storm surge.
3. A bar graph showing percentage of total flooded land by land-cover type.
4. A map showing infrastructure and health facility destruction.
5. A table showing various land types that were flooded measured in acres and square miles.

Examine the data

The data for this project is stored in the **OurWorld4\Module4\Project2\data** folder.

Reminder

You can explore the metadata in ArcCatalog. The table on the following page helps you organize this information.

Q1 *Investigate the metadata and complete this table on your worksheet:*

Layer	Data Type	Publication Information: Who Created The Data?	Time Period Data Is Relevant	Spatial Horizontal Coordinate System	Attribute Values	Resolution For Rasters
airports	Vector				N/A	N/A
keywest					N/A	N/A
elev			1999		Elevation is expressed in meters	1 arc second 0.000369 30 meters
ghospitals				Geographic	N/A	N/A
kw_places	Vector	Author Created Data	2007	Geographic	N/A	N/A
landcover	Raster		2003			1 arc second 0.000369 30 meters
usa_ streets	Vector				N/A	N/A

Organize and document your work

Reminder

- Set up the proper directory structure.
- Create a process summary.
- Document the map.
- Set the data frame properties for each project. Since none of the data used in this project is projected, set the coordinate system to be UTM 1983 Zone 17N in the Data Frame Properties window. This map projection is appropriate for the Key West region and the unit of measurement is meters. Setting the projection will ensure the most accurate calculations in ArcMap.
- Set the environments:
  a. Set the Working Directory.
  b. Set the Scratch Directory.
  c. Set the Output Coordinate System to "Same as Display."
  d. Set the Extent to Same as Layer Keywest.
  e. Set the Output Cell Size to 30.
  f. Set the Mask to Keywest.

Analysis

An important first step in GIS analysis is to develop a basemap of your study area. Complete deliverable 1 and answer the questions below to orient yourself to the study area.

▶ **Deliverable 1: Map of elevation and bathymetry of Key West with Key West places labeled and streets displayed.**

Q2 *What is the highest elevation shown?*

Q3 *What are the places that are extremely vulnerable to flooding?*

Q4 *What different types of coastal land are represented?*

The next step is to determine what land was flooded by the storm surge and to plot the flooded land by land-cover type. Complete deliverables 2 and 3 and answer the questions to conduct this analysis.

▶ **Deliverable 2: A map of flooded land in Key West after the Wilma storm surge.**

▶ **Deliverable 3: A bar graph showing percentage of total flooded land by land-cover type.**

1. Refer to your process summary for project 1 if you forgot how to do the analysis.

2. Reclassify the land-cover values as follows:

Old Values	Label	New Values
11	Water	1
21,22,23	Developed	2
31	Barren	3
51,61,71	Scrub/Grass	4
91,92	Wetlands	5

Q5 *What type of land was most flooded?*

Q6 *Describe the flooding of Key West.*

3. Calculate the percentage of land cover by type [Reminder: PERCENT = (COUNT/Sum of COUNT*100)]. You do not want to include the pixels for the land that was not flooded.

Q7 *Record the sum of the COUNT field (excluding not flooded land).*

4. Make a bar graph of the percentage of land cover by type.

Q8 *What does the graph tell you about the greatest impact of the storm surge?*

Q9 *Describe the distribution of the flooded areas and how the flood might affect the long-term sustainability of the region.*

You also need a map showing what hospitals and other important parts of the Key West infrastructure are under threat from the storm.

▶ **Deliverable 4: A map showing infrastructure and health facilities at risk from the storm surge.**

Q10 *What is the distribution of infrastructure and health facilities affected by the storm surge and how might you prioritize which damaged elements should be restored first?*

The final piece of the puzzle is to determine the area of the different land types flooded.

▶ **Deliverable 5: A table showing various land types that were flooded measured in acres and square miles.**

Reminder

1. The field type should be float.
2. ACRES = COUNT * 900 /4046.68.
3. SQUARE MILES = ACRES/640.

Q11 *Complete this table on your worksheet:*

Type	Acres	Square Miles
Not Flooded		
Water		
Developed		
Barren		
Scrub/Grass		
Wetlands		

Presentation

Remember to keep in mind the interests and expertise of your audience as you prepare your presentation. Remember to develop a solution to the original problem and present your results in a compelling way.

Module 4: Project 3 ● ● ○

On your own

You've worked through a guided activity on the impact of hurricanes on a coastal area and repeated that analysis in another community. In this section you will reinforce the skills you've developed by researching and analyzing a similar scenario entirely on your own. First you must identify your study area and acquire data for your analysis. A list of possible storms (and their impact areas) are suggested below. However, if there is another storm that has significant interest to you (perhaps one that has affected your area), download and work with that data.

- New Orleans/Katrina
- Mississippi (or Appalachian Valley)/Camille
- Florida/Camille
- Charleston, South Carolina/Andrew
- Gulf Coast/Rita
- Wilmington, North Carolina/Fran

Refer to your process summary and the preceding module projects if you need help. Here are some basic steps to help you organize your work:

Research

Research the particular event and answer the following questions:

1. What is the area of study?
2. What is the extent of the storm surge or flooding?
3. What were the critical issues of the event?

Obtain the data

Do you have access to baseline data? The ESRI Data and Maps Media Kit provides many of the layers of data that are needed for project work. Be sure to pay particular attention to the source of each data layer and get the latest version. Also use the StreetMap USA database for accurate street data, if you need it.

If you do not have access to The ESRI Data and Maps Media Kit, you can obtain data from the following sources:

- http://www.esri.com/tiger
- http://www.geographynetwork.com
- http://www.nationalatlas.gov

Workflow

After researching the problem and obtaining the data, you should do the following:

1. Write a brief scenario.
2. State the problem.
3. Define the deliverables.
4. Examine the data using ArcCatalog.
5. Set the directory structure, start your process summary, and document the map.
6. Decide what you need for the data frame coordinate system and the environments.
    a. What is the best projection for your work?
    b. Do you need to set a cell size or mask?
7. Start your analysis.
8. Prepare your presentation and deliverables.

Always remember to document your work in a process summary.

MODULE 5

Location decisions

Introduction

There's an abundance of spatial data available to help answer where questions. Where should I buy a house? Where should I establish my business? GIS can help you gather, analyze, and visualize data to create reliable location intelligence that results in sound decisions. In this module, you will apply similar GIS processes for completely different purposes. Although the scenarios are fictitious, the locations and the data are real. You will study the rapidly growing area of Maricopa County, Arizona, to find a home for a doctor and a teacher with specific requirements. Then, in project two, the scene shifts to Ohio where the task at hand is to find the perfect spot for the fictitious Central Ohio College for the Arts' student radio station. In this module, you will examine census data and work with weighted overlays. These spatial skills can be applied to countless siting decisions large and small.

Projects in this module:

- **Homing in on Maricopa County, Arizona**

- **Station location in Franklin County, Ohio**

- **On your own**

Module worksheets

The student worksheet files can be found on the Data and Resources DVD.

Project 1 student sheet

- File name: Maricopa_student_worksheet.doc
- Location: OurWorld4\Module5\Project1\documents
- Document length: 5 pages
- Worksheet for "Homing in on Maricopa County, Arizona." A form for answering questions, completing tables, and tracking work to be handed in.

Project 2 student sheet

- File name: Franklin_student_worksheet.doc
- Location: OurWorld4\Module5\Project2\documents
- Document length: 2 pages
- Worksheet for "Station location in Franklin County, Ohio." A form for answering questions, completing tables, and tracking work to be handed in.

Homing in on Maricopa County, Arizona

Scenario

Choosing a place to live is a complicated decision influenced by many factors. You need to balance your personal preferences with work, budget, and family constraints. In this exercise, you will make decisions about where to live using demographic data, property information, and such spatial factors as proximity to important landmarks. You can prioritize your preferences by giving some factors more weight than others.

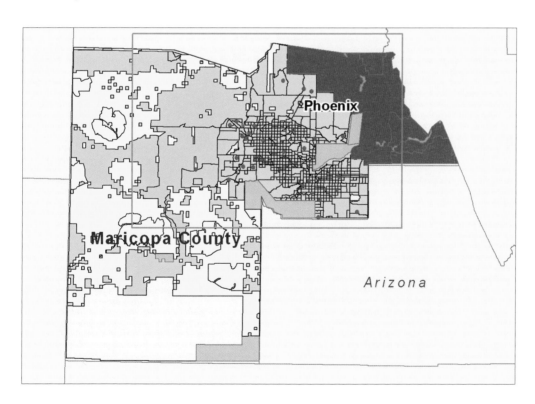

Maricopa County, Arizona, is the fourteenth largest county in the United States, covering 9,224 square miles, and the fourth most populous with more than 3.7 million people. More than 60 percent of the people in Arizona live in Maricopa County. Phoenix is the county seat and other cities include Mesa, Glendale, Scottsdale, Tempe, Chandler, Peoria, and Gilbert. These cities are close to each other and make up most of the state's metropolitan area. The remainder of the county contains a large amount of federal and Indian land.

Problem

A couple—a pediatrician and a college professor—landed jobs in Maricopa County. She has accepted a position at Chandler Regional Hospital and he plans to teach at Phoenix College. They have listed four priorities about where they want to live:

- Close to Chandler Regional Hospital
- Close to Phoenix College
- A neighborhood with a high percentage of people 40 to 49 years old
- A neighborhood with high house values

In applying GIS to a problem, you must have a very clear understanding of the problem or scenario. We find it helpful to answer these four questions, which test your understanding and divide the problem into smaller problems that are easier to solve.

Q1 *What geographic area are you studying? (Record answers on your worksheet.)*

Q2 *What decisions do you need to make?*

Q3 *What information would help you make the decision?*

Q4 *Who are the key stakeholders for this issue? (This step is important. You need to know the audience for your analysis to help decide how to present your results.)*

Deliverables

After identifying the problem you're trying to solve, you need to envision the kinds of data displays (maps, graphs, and tables) that will address the problem. We recommend the following deliverables for this exercise:

1. A basemap of Maricopa County showing places, federal land, and Indian reservations.
2. One map showing the following parameters:
   - Distance from Chandler Regional Hospital
   - Distance from Phoenix College
   - Census tracts with percentage of people 40–49
   - Census tracts showing median house value
3. A map showing two weighted overlays combining the various factors with a paragraph about the pros and cons of each analysis.

Examine the data

The next step in your workflow is to identify, collect, and examine the data for the locational analysis. Here, we've identified and collected the data you will need. Explore the data to discover information the various layers contain.

You will use ArcCatalog to preview the GIS data and explore the metadata associated with each feature class.

1. Open ArcCatalog and connect to the folder **OurWorld4\Module5\Project1\ data**.

2. Expand the data folder in the Catalog tree and double-click the Location geodatabase.

3. Click the Preview tab, then preview the geography and table for each feature class in the geodatabase.

The spatial coordinate system, the resolution of the data, and the attributes are all important pieces of information about each data layer. You need this information for your analysis. Fortunately, the metadata associated with each layer allows you to easily access this information.

Q5 *Investigate the metadata and complete this table on your worksheet:*

Layer	Data Type	Publication Information: Who Created The Data?	Time Period Data Is Relevant	Spatial Horizontal Coordinate System	Attribute Values
places					Demographic Data
schools					
sel_tracts					

4. Close ArcCatalog.

Now that you've explored the available data, you're almost ready to begin your analysis. First you need to start a process summary, document your project, and set the project environments.

Organize and document your work

Step 1: Examine the directory structure

The next phase in a GIS project is to carefully keep track of the data and your calculations. You will work with a number of different files and it is important to keep them organized so you can easily find them. The best way to do this is to have a folder for your project that contains a data folder. For this project, the folder called **OurWorld4\Module5\Project1** will be your project folder. Make sure that it is stored in a place where you have write access. You can store your data inside the results folder. The results folder already contains an empty geodatabase named **project1_results**. Save your map documents inside the **OurWorld4\Module5\Project1\results** folder.

Step 2: Create a process summary

The process summary is just a list of the steps you used to do your analysis. We suggest using a simple text document for your process summary. Keep adding to it as you do your work to avoid forgetting any steps. The list below shows an example of the first few entries in a process summary:

1. Explore the data.
2. Produce a basemap of Maricopa County.
3. Calculate the distance from Chandler Regional Hospital.
4. Reclassify the distance from Chandler Regional Hospital.

Step 3: Document the map

You need to add descriptive properties to every map document you produce. Use the same descriptive properties listed below for every map document in the module or individualize the documentation from map to map.

1. Open ArcMap and save the map document as **location1**. (Save it in the **OurWorld4\Module5\Project1\results** folder.)

2. From the File menu, choose Document Properties and in the dialog box add a title, author, and some descriptive text.

Title:	Homing in on Maricopa County, Arizona
Subject:	Site Selection
Author:	Kathryn Keranen and Bob Kolvoord
Category:	Social Science
Keywords:	site selection, weighted overlay
Comments:	A housing site selection will be determined based on established parameters. Scale and rank will be assigned and various scenarios proposed.
Hyperlink base:	
Template:	Normal.mxt

☐ Save thumbnail image with map

Data Source Options...

3. Click Data Source Options and then click the radio button to store relative paths of data sources. Click OK in both dialog boxes.

Storing relative paths for data sources allows ArcMap to automatically find all relevant data if you move your project folder to a new location or computer.

Step 4: Set the environments

In GIS analysis, you will often get data from various sources and this data may be in different coordinate systems and/or map projections. When using GIS to perform area calculations, you would like your result to be in familiar units, such as miles or kilometers. Data in an unprojected geographic coordinate system has units of decimal degrees, which are difficult to interpret. Thus, your calculations will be more meaningful if all the feature classes involved are in the same map projection. Fortunately, ArcMap can do much of this work for you if you set certain environment variables and data frame properties. In this step, you'll learn how to change these settings.

To display your data correctly, you'll need to set the coordinate system for the data frame. When you add data with a defined coordinate system, ArcMap will automatically set the data frame's projection to match the data. If you add subsequent layers that have a coordinate system different from the data frame, they are automatically projected on-the-fly to the data frame's coordinate system. In this exercise, data will automatically project to match the UTM projection for Arizona.

1. From the View menu, choose Data Frame Properties. Click the Coordinate System tab. Expand Predefined, expand Projected Coordinate Systems, expand UTM, expand NAD 1983, select Zone 12N, and click OK. If necessary, click OK again to set the projection.

Before using ArcToolbox tools to make your calculations, you will establish some general environment settings that apply to all of the tools you'll be using. The analysis environment includes the workspace where results will be placed, and the extent, cell size, and coordinate system for the results.

2. Open ArcToolbox, right-click any empty space within ArcToolbox and choose Environments.

3. Expand General Settings.

By default, inputs and outputs are placed in your current workspace, but you can redirect the output to another workspace such as your results folder.

4. Set the Current Workspace as **OurWorld4\Module5\Project1\data\ Location.gdb**.

5. Set the Scratch Workspace as **OurWorld4\Module5\Project1\results\ project1_results.gdb**.

6. For Output Coordinate System, select "Same as Display."

7. Set the Extent to sel_tracts (sel_tracts can be found in the Location.gdb in the data folder).

8. Expand Raster Analysis Settings.

You also want to limit your analysis to the selected census tracts in Maricopa County. This is accomplished by using an analysis mask. The mask identifies those locations within the analysis extent that will be included when using a tool.

9. Set the cell size to 300.

10. Set the Mask to sel_tracts.

11. Click OK.

Analysis

Once you've examined the data, completed map documentation, and set the environments, you are ready to begin the analysis and to prepare the displays you need to address the problem. A good place to start any GIS analysis is to produce a locational or basemap to better understand the distribution of features in the geographic area you're studying. First, you will prepare a basemap of Maricopa County showing places and federal lands.

Step 1: Create a basemap of Maricopa County

1. Add county.

2. Add fedland and symbolize it with Unique Value using the AGBUR field.

   - *BIA: Bureau of Indian Affairs*
   - *BLM: Bureau of Land Management*
   - *BOR: Bureau of Reclamation*
   - *DOD: Department of Defense*
   - *FS: Forest Service*
   - *NPS: National Park Service*

3. Add places.

4. Add sel_tracts. The sel_tracts is the area of interest for the study.

▶ **Deliverable 1: A basemap of Maricopa County showing places, federal land, and Indian reservations.**

5. Save the map document.

The following steps require the ArcGIS Spatial Analyst extension to be installed and turned on. Before beginning, open ArcMap and from the Tools menu, select Extensions and check Spatial Analyst.

Step 2: Calculate distance from Chandler Regional Hospital

1. Open a new map document and save it as **location2**.

2. Refer back to "Organize and document your work" and do the following:

   a. *Document the map.*
   b. *Set the data frame properties. They must be set for each data frame.*
   c. *Set the environments.*

3. Add sel_tracts

Sel_tracts is a subset of all of the county's census tracts and shows only the census tracts used to determine where the family will live.

4. Add hospitals.

5. Select Chandler Regional Hospital.

6. Right-click hospitals, select Data and click Export Data to export the selected hospital as CRH to project1_results.gdb. Save the file as a File and Personal Geodatabase feature class.

7. Remove hospitals.

8. Label Chandler Regional Hospital in CRH.

9. Open ArcToolbox, expand Spatial Analyst Tools and then expand Distance. Double-click Euclidean Distance.

10. Input CRH and name the output raster **dist_hosp**. Set the cell size to 300.

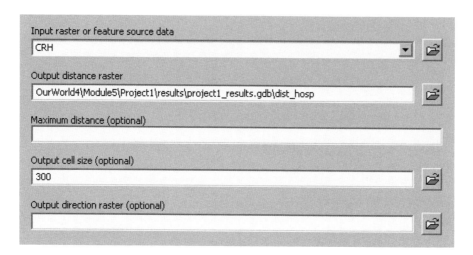

11. Click OK.

12. Turn off sel_tracts.

Q6 *What do the different colors mean?*

Q7 *In what unit are measurements reported and how do you know?*

Q8 *Click the measuring tool. From the drop-down menu within the measuring tool, select Distance and then Miles. Using the Measuring tool, measure the color bands. How many miles does each color band represent?*

In the rest of the project, you will be using a software function that only accepts whole numbers. You will reclassify the distance data into nine classes.

13. Open ArcToolbox, expand Spatial Analyst tools and expand Reclass. Double-click Reclassify.

14. The input raster is dist_hosp.

15. Click the Classify button and change the classification method to Defined Interval. For interval size, type **10000** and click OK.

16. Change any of the New Values that are greater than 9 to 9.

17. Name the output raster **reclass_hosp**.

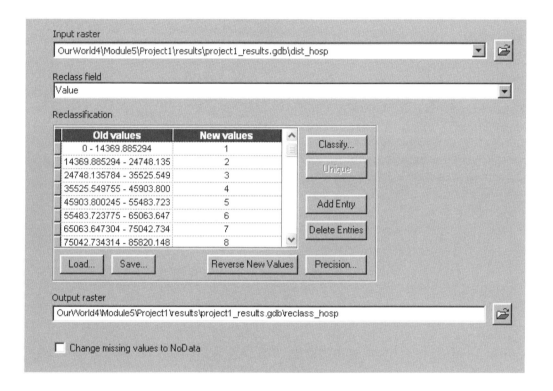

18. Click OK.

19. Remove dist_hosp.

20. Select an appropriate color scheme for reclass_hosp. Remember, the closer to the hospital the better for this couple's housing.

21. Turn sel_tracts back on and make them hollow.

22. Name the data frame **hospital distance**.

23. Save the map document.

Q9 *Which value is closest to the hospital, 1 or 9?*

Step 3: Calculate distance from Phoenix College

1. Insert a new data frame and name it **college distance**. Remember to set the coordinate system in the data frame properties.

2. Add sel_tracts.

3. Add schools.

4. Select Phoenix College.

5. Export the selection as PC as you did above with the hospital.

6. Remove schools.

7. Label Phoenix College in PC.

8. Open ArcToolbox, expand Spatial Analyst tools, and then expand Distance. Double-click Euclidean Distance. The input raster should be PC and the output raster dist_school. Set the cell size to 300.

9. Click OK.

10. Turn off sel_tracts.

11. Open ArcToolbox and Expand Spatial Analyst tools and expand Reclass. Double-click Reclassify.

12. The input raster is dist_school.

13. Click the Classify button and change the classification method to Defined Interval. For interval size, type **10000** and click OK.

14. Name the output raster **reclass_sch**.

15. Click OK.

16. Remove dist_school.

17. Select an appropriate color scheme for reclass_sch. Remember, the closer to the school the better.

18. Turn sel_tracts back on and make them hollow.

19. Save the map document.

Q10 *Which value is closest to the school, 1 or 8?*

Step 4: Create a field for percentage of population 40–49

The population density of people 40-49 in each census tract is represented as a percentage of the total population, so a permanent field in the sel_tracts attribute table needs to be created that shows this percentage.

1. Insert a new data frame and name it **Age 40–49**. Remember to set the coordinate system in the data frame properties.

2. Add sel_tracts.

3. Open the sel_tracts attribute table and click Options and select Add Field.

4. Name the new field **percent**. Set the field type as float. Click OK.

5. Right-click the new percent field and select Field Calculator. Perform the following calculation: AGE_40_49/POP2000 * 100.

6. Click OK.

7. Display sel_tracts by Graduated colors with the Value Field percent.

Q11 *Are there any tracts that have 0 percent? Why or why not?*

Q12 *Are there clusters of census tracts that have a higher percentage of population 40–49?*

Q13 *How can a census tract have 100 percent population age 40-49?*

8. Save your map document.

Step 5: Convert tracts to a raster for age range and reclassify

To calculate your final decision, all of the data layers must be either vector or raster feature classes. In this exercise, it is easier to use rasters. Fortunately, polygon vector feature classes can be easily converted to rasters with the value of the chosen attribute from the polygon feature class.

1. Open ArcToolbox, expand Conversion Tools and expand To Raster. Double-click Feature to Raster.

2. The input feature should be sel_tracts and the field should be percent.

3. The output raster should be named **rightage** and the output cell size set to 300.

4. Click OK.

5. Turn off sel_tracts.

6. Open ArcToolbox, expand Spatial Analyst tools and expand Reclass. Double-click Reclassify.

7. The input raster is rightage.

8. Name the output raster **rec_rightage**.

9. Click OK.

10. Select an appropriate color scheme for rec_rightage.

11. Remove rightage.

12. Display sel_tracts by single symbol and make it hollow.

13. Add PC and CRH, then symbolize and label each feature.

14. Save the map document.

Step 6: Find median house values

In this step, data preparation requires an Internet connection, an Internet browser, and Microsoft Excel. You need to download the house values from the U.S. Census Bureau Web site and then join the values to sel_tracts in order to include them in your analysis.

A. Download data from U.S. Census Bureau and join to sel_tracts

1. Go to http://www.factfinder.census.gov.

2. On the left side of the page click DATA SETS.

3. Under the heading 2000, click the radio button beside Census 2000 Summary File 3 (SF 3) – Sample Data.

4. After checking the radio button, click Detailed Tables.

5. Under geographic type, select Census Tract.

6. Under Select a state, select Arizona.

7. Under Select a county, select Maricopa County.

8. Under Select one or more geographic areas, choose All Census Tracts and click Add. Don't forget to click Add.

9. When all the census tracts populate the Current geography selections box, click Next.

10. The table that shows median house value is H76. Median Value (Dollars) for Specified Owner-Occupied Housing Units. Choose that table and click Add.

11. Click Show Result.

12. At the top of the page there is a Print/Download Tab. Click Download.

13. When the next page appears, scroll down and check the Microsoft Excel (.xls) radio button.

14. Click OK and Save to Disk.

15. Unzip the downloaded data file.

16. Open dt_dec_2000_sf3_u_data1 in Microsoft Excel. The table should have more than 600 rows.

17. This table has two columns you need to join to sel_tracts: The Geography Identifier (GEO_ID2), which is actually the FIPS (Federal Information Processing Standard) number, and the Specified owner_occupied housing units: Median value. Delete all the columns except those two.

18. Delete the First Row.

19. Change Geography Identifier to FIPS.

20. Change Specified owner-occupied housing units: Median value to median_val.

	A	B
1	FIPS	median_val
2	04013010100	398000
3	04013020201	84700
4	04013020202	73500
5	04013030302	99900
6	04013030303	89600
7	04013030304	132800
8	04013030307	96900

21. Save the spreadsheet as **house_val**.

B. Join the data

1. In ArcMap, insert a New Data Frame and name it **Median House Value**. Remember to set the coordinate system in the data frame properties.

2. Add sel_tracts.

3. Add the spreadsheet file house_val.xls by clicking the Add Data button, navigating to house_val.xls, double-clicking it, and then clicking Sheet0$. Click Add.

4. Right-click sel_tracts, choose Join and Relates, and select Join.

5. Choose the field in this layer that the join will be based on: FIPS.

6. The software should automatically find the spreadsheet Sheet0$ and the field FIPS (if not, select them in the appropriate menus).

7. Click OK.

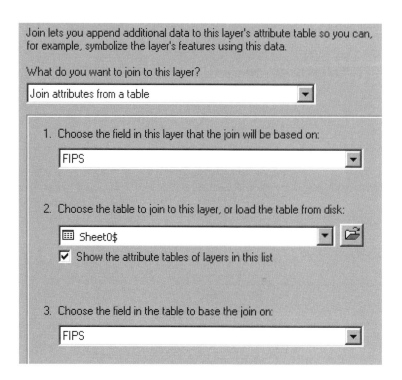

C. Clean up the data

In this section you want to get rid of any tracts that did not join with the census data (NULL) or any tracts with a value of 0 for median house value. This will facilitate our analysis.

1. Open the attribute table of sel_tracts.

2. Right-click Sheet0$.Median_val and select Sort Ascending.

3. Highlight the rows that contain NULL or 0 by pressing the control key as you select the rows. You should select 13 rows out of the 660 present.

4. Go to Options and Switch Selection.

5. Close the attribute table.

6. Right-click sel_tracts and choose Data and select Export Data.

7. Export the file as **median_val** and put it in your results folder.

8. Remove sel_tracts.

9. Remove Sheet0$.

D. Change median_val to a raster and reclassify

1. Open ArcToolbox, expand Conversion Tools and Expand To Raster. Double-click Feature to Raster.

2. The input feature should be median_val and the field should be median_val.

3. The output raster should be named house_val and the cell size set to 300.

4. Click OK.

5. Remove median_val.

6. Open ArcToolbox, expand Spatial Analyst tools, and expand Reclass. Double-click Reclassify.

7. The input raster should be set to house_val and the output raster should be set to **rec_val**.

8. Click OK.

9. Select an appropriate color scheme for rec_val.

10. Remove house_val.

11. Add sel_tracts and make the symbol hollow.

12. Add PC and CRH, symbolize and label each feature.

13. Create a presentation layout showing all four Data Frames.

14. Save the map document.

Q14 *Where is the median house value highest?*

▶ Deliverable 2: A map showing the following parameters:
- Distance from Chandler Regional Hospital
- Distance from Phoenix College
- Census tracts with percentage of people 40–49
- Census tracts showing median house value

Now that you have created feature classes and converted them to rasters, you are ready to combine them for a weighted overlay map to identify the optimal locations for this couple's house.

When you use a weighted overlay, you can assign both rank and weight to your data. Use a scale of 1-9 to rank each of our layers, with 1 being the worst choice and 9 being the best choice. After you rank your data, you will give a weight based on the importance of that data in your analysis.

Step 7: Create a weighted overlay with each factor weighted at 25 percent

In your first overlay, each factor will have same weight in the decision (4 factors, 25 percent each). In this step, you will use ArcGIS ModelBuilder. This tool allows you to run different scenarios and make decisions using both rank and scale.

1. Open a new blank map document and save it as **location3**.

2. Refer back to "Organize and document your work" and do the following:

    a. *Document the map.*

    b. *Set the data frame properties. They must be set for each data frame.*

    c. *Set the environments.*

3. Add reclass_hosp, reclass_schl, rec_rightage, and rec_val. Choose appropriate symbology for each layer.

4. Open ArcToolbox. Right-click in the white space in ArcToolbox and choose New Toolbox. The new toolbox will appear at the bottom of the ArcToolbox window.

5. Right-click your new toolbox and select New/Model to create a new model.

6. Drag reclass_hosp, reclass_sch, rec_rightage, and rec_val into the model window.

7. In your first overlay, each factor will have the same weight in the decisions (4 factors, 25 percent each). Open Spatial Analyst Tools > Overlay. Drag the process Weighted Overlay into the ModelBuilder window.

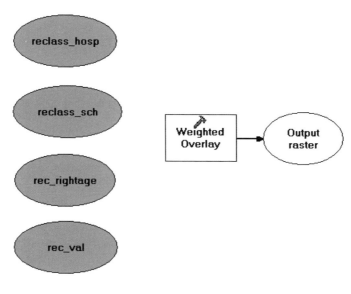

8. Connect all the files (reclass_hosp, reclass_sch, rec_rightage, and rec_val) to the process Weighted Overlay with the Add Connection tool. Click the Table (Parameter) if required.

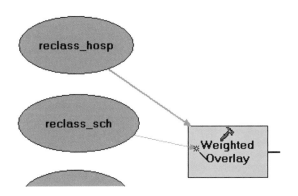

9. Double-click the Weighted Overlay Process to open the Weighted Overlay Menu.

When you study the weighted overlay table, you see that the function allows the calculation of a multiple criteria analysis with a number of raster feature classes. It allows the calculation of percentage influence as well as scale value.

Q15 *For this first scenario, what should the percentage influence be?*

Q16 *What is the scale value?*

10. The first file you will deal with is reclass_hosp.

Q17 *What is the couple's priority concerning the hospital?*

Q18 *How do the distance values vary from the hospital moving outward?*

After answering the questions above, note that the scale value needs to be reversed.

11. Click the arrow under Scale Value and it will reverse the scale. Now the closest distance to the hospital has the highest rank.

12. Collapse the file by clicking the double arrows on the left side of the file name.

13. Repeat this procedure for the reclass_sch.

14. Look at rec_rightage. The scale value is correct for rec_rightage. The census tracts with the highest percentage of people 40–49 has the highest value.

15. Collapse rec_rightage.

16. Look at rec_val. The scale value is correct for rec_val. The census tracts with the highest house values have the highest value.

17. Collapse rec_val.

18. Give each of the layers a weight of 25 percent by entering **25** for each layer under % Influence.

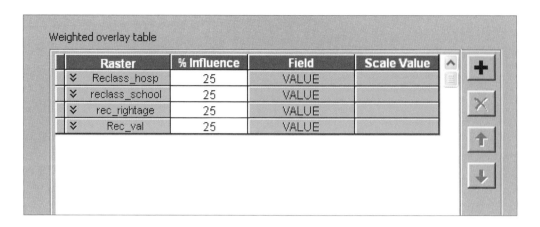

Weighted overlay table

	Raster	% Influence	Field	Scale Value
≽	Reclass_hosp	25	VALUE	
≽	reclass_school	25	VALUE	
≽	rec_rightage	25	VALUE	
≽	Rec_val	25	VALUE	

19. Name the output raster **weight1** and put it in your results geodatabase.

20. Click OK.

21. Click the Run Model Icon to run the model and do the calculations.

22. Right-click weight1 in the model and select Add to Display.

23. Close the model and save changes.

24. Select an appropriate color ramp for weight1.

25. The place that best fits all the parameters is the section with the highest value (6 or 7).

26. Make those values an appropriate color.

27. Add places.

28. Label the places nearest the areas that best fit the criteria.

29. Add sel_tracts and make it hollow.

30. Add CRH and PC, and symbolize and label them appropriately.

31. Select three census tracts that best meet the criteria and designate those areas with an appropriate graphic symbol.

32. Name the data frame **weighted overlay 1**.

33. Save your map document.

Step 8: Create a second weighted overlay

After the couple visited Maricopa County and were overwhelmed by the traffic, they changed their minds about the influence each factor should have. They decided on the following weights for the different criteria:

- Close to hospital: 40%
- Close to college: 40%
- Age 40–49: 10%
- Median house value: 10%

1. Insert a new data frame and name it **weighted overlay 2**.

If you closed your model, right-click the model, select Edit, and the model will open.

2. Open the Weighted Overlay Process in your model and change the values to reflect the weights shown above.

3. Name the new file **weight2**.

4. Run the model.

5. Add weight2 to the display.

6. The places that best fit all the parameters are the sections of the raster with the highest value.

7. Add places.

8. Label the places nearest the areas that best fit the criteria.

9. Add the sel_tracts layer and make it hollow.

10. Add CRH and PC, and symbolize and label them.

11. Select three census tracts that best meet the criteria and designate those areas with an appropriate graphic symbol.

12. Prepare a layout showing both data frames.

Q19 *Explain the pros and cons of each analysis.*

13. Save the map document.

▶ Deliverable 3: A map showing two weighted overlays combining the various factors with a paragraph about the pros and cons of each analysis.

Once your analysis is complete, you're not done. You still need to develop a solution to the original problem and present your results in a compelling way to the pediatrician and professor in this particular situation. The presentation of your various data displays must explain what they show and how they contribute to solving the problem.

Presentation

Write a paragraph explaining the differences between the two weighted overlays and your recommendations for the couple's house search. Pay particular attention to how changing the percentage influence affected the outcome. Remember that your audience probably lacks your in-depth knowledge of GIS, so you'll need to communicate your results without using technical jargon and explain the importance of the various deliverables.

M ● ● ● ● ●
P ● ○ ○

Station location in Franklin County, Ohio

Scenario

Students from Central Ohio College for the Arts (COCA) visited Ohio State University (OSU). While they were at OSU, they listened to the LPFM (Low Power FM) campus radio station, which sparked an interest to start their own station. These noncommercial educational stations operate at up to 100 watts with about a 3.5-mile radius service range (http://www.fcc.gov/mb/audio/lpfm/index.html). The students learned from radio station personnel that the OSU LPFM campus station was run by students, aired noncommercial musical selections, carried local sports and news, and broadcast emergency announcements. The station provided an opportunity for professional radio training and allowed disc jockeys to play different styles of music. Central Ohio College for the Arts decided to apply to the Federal Communications Commission (FCC) for a license.

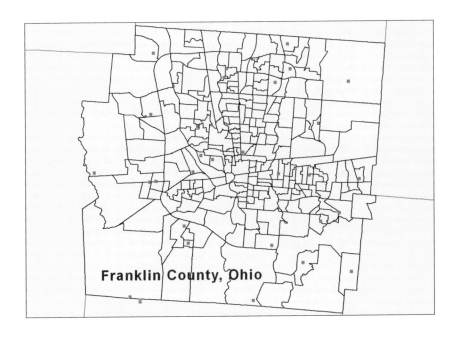

Franklin County, Ohio

Problem

Before they applied to the FCC, the students wanted to consider alternative sites for the station. They used the following criteria to determine acceptable locations:

- High percentage of the population between 18–29
- Close to the Central Ohio College for the Arts campus
- Away from Ohio State University

Reminder

It helps to divide a large problem such as this into a set of smaller tasks such as the following:

- Identify the geographic study area.
- Determine the sequence of steps in your study.
- Identify the decisions to be made.
- Develop the information required to make decisions.
- Identify stakeholders for this issue.

Deliverables

We recommend the following deliverables for this exercise:

1. A basemap of Franklin County census tracts showing Ohio State University and Central Ohio College for the Arts.
2. A single layout showing a map of each of the following parameters:
   - Distance from Central Ohio College for the Arts
   - Distance from Ohio State University
   - Census tracts with percentage of population 18–29
3. A map showing two different weighted overlays.

Examine the data

The data for this project is stored in the **OurWorld4\Module5\Project2\data** folder.

Reminder

You can explore the metadata in ArcCatalog. The table on the following page helps you organize this information.

Q1 *Investigate the metadata and complete this table on your worksheet:*

Layer	Data Type	Publication Information: Who Created The Data?	Time Period Data Is Relevant	Spatial Horizontal Coordinate System	Attribute For Vectors
schools					Name
places					Demographic Data
tracts					

Organize and document your work

Reminder

- Set up the proper directory structure.
- Create a process summary.
- Document the map.
- Set the environments:
  a. Set the Data Frame Properties Coordinate System to UTM 1983 Zone 17N.
  b. Set the Working Directory.
  c. Set the Scratch Directory.
  d. Set the Output Coordinate System to "Same as Display."
  e. Set the Extent to Same As Layer Tracts.
  f. Set the Output Cell Size to 150.
  g. Set the Mask to tracts.

Analysis

An important first step in GIS analysis is to develop a basemap of your study area. Complete deliverable 1 and answer the questions below to orient yourself to the study area.

▶ **Deliverable 1: A basemap of Franklin County census tracts showing Ohio State University and Central Ohio College for the Arts.**

Continuing your analysis, make distance maps from Central Ohio College for the Arts and Ohio State University. For distances from OSC and COCA, reclassify using a defined interval of 4,500 meters.

1. Refer to your process summary to produce a raster showing percentage of population between 18 and 29. To calculate the percentage of 18–29, you must add the 18–21 and the 22–29 fields and then divide by POP2000. The field calculation should be as follows:

   ([AGE_18_21] + [AGE_22_29]) / [POP2000]

2. Reclassify the 18–29 population using a defined interval of 0.12.

▶ **Deliverable 2: A single layout showing a map of each of the following parameters:**

   • **Distance from Central Ohio College for the Arts**
   • **Distance from Ohio State University**
   • **Census tracts with percentage of population 18–29**

The next deliverable consists of assigning scale and rank to create the weighted overlays.

Reminder

The ranking needs to be reversed for the distance from Central Ohio College for the Arts. Locations closer to COCA should have a higher rank than locations farther away.

▶ **Deliverable 3: A map showing two weighted overlays.**

The first should be weighted as follows:

   • Age 18–29: 34%
   • Distance from OSU: 33%
   • Close to COCA: 33%

The second should be weighted as follows:

   • Age 18–29: 25%
   • Distance from OSU: 25%
   • Close to COCA: 50%

Q2 *Discuss the two weighted overlays.*

Try some different weighting schemes and discuss the results. Are there other decision criteria you might want to include?

Presentation

Remember to keep in mind the interests and expertise of your audience as you prepare your presentation. Remember to develop a solution to the original problem and present your results in a compelling way.

Module 5: Project 3 ● ● ● ○

On your own

You've worked through a guided activity on choosing locations based on weighted decision making for a couple choosing a location to live and you've repeated that analysis for the siting of a radio station. In this section, you will reinforce the skills you've developed by researching and analyzing a similar scenario entirely on your own. First, you must identify your study area and acquire data for your analysis. Four possible siting problems that require weighted decision making are suggested below. However, if there is another problem that has significant interest to you (perhaps one that affects your area), download and work with that data.

- A new school
- A county landfill
- A new hospital
- A retirement community

Refer to your process summary and the preceding module projects if you need help. Here are some basic steps to help you organize your work:

Research

Research the problem and answer the following questions:

1. What is the area of study?
2. What is the siting problem and what are the decision constraints?

Obtain the data

Do you have access to baseline data? The ESRI Data and Maps Media Kit provides many of the layers of data that are needed for project work. Be sure to pay particular attention to the source of data and get the latest version.

If you do not have access to The ESRI Data and Maps Media Kit, you can obtain data from the following sources:

- http://www.esri.com/tiger
- http://www.geographynetwork.com
- http://www.nationalatlas.gov

Workflow

After researching the problem and obtaining the data, you should do the following:

1. Write a brief scenario.
2. State the problem.
3. Define the deliverables.
4. Examine the data using ArcCatalog.
5. Set the directory structure, start your process summary, and document the map.
6. Decide what you need for the data frame coordinate system and the environments.
   a. What is the best projection for your work?
   b. Do you need to set a cell size or mask?
7. Start your analysis.
8. Prepare your presentation and deliverables.

Always remember to document your work in a process summary.

Create a network database

To establish routes that avoid obstacles or to find the shortest distance between two points, ArcMap requires you to create a network from shapefiles that contain edges, junctions, turns, and speed. The directions to create such a database follow:

1. Clip the desired street feature class from streetmap_usa from the ESRI Data and Maps 2006 Media Kit.

2. Open ArcCatalog.

3. On the Tools menu, click Extensions and click Network Analyst to turn on the extension.

4. Right-click the usastreets shapefile and choose New Network Dataset.

5. The name of the network dataset is usastreets_ND by default.

6. Click Next.

7. Click Next and select the default connectivity settings.

8. Click Next to accept No to the elevation field data.

9. Click Next to accept Yes to model turns in this network.

10. Click Next to specify attributes for the network dataset and click Yes to add one cost based on the shape length.

11. Click Next to establish driving direction settings.

12. Click Finish.

13. Once created, the system prompts for the network to be built. Click Yes to build the network.

14. The usastreets_ND is added to ArcCatalog along with the system junctions.

15. Close ArcCatalog.

Cartographic information

ESRI provides mapmaking novices with practical instruction on how to produce effective displays. "Introduction to Map Design" covers such topics as types of maps, scale, projections, generalization, symbolization, composition, and accuracy. You can access "Introduction to Map Design" in the Resources folder on your DVD as intrcart.pdf or through this link:

http://www.esri.com/industries/k-12/download/docs/intrcart.pdf

Also, visit the ESRI Mapping Center online at http://mappingcenter.esri.com/.

This site is a central repository for "the use of ArcGIS in the graphic delivery of geographic information." It is a great resource for tips on cartography and using ArcGIS to make high-quality maps.

Resources

Helpful Web sites

http://edcommunity.esri.com/
The ESRI Education Community Portal serves as a portal for educational users. It promotes connections between GIS users at all education levels and describes innovative uses of GIS.

http://rockyweb.cr.usgs.gov/outreach/rockylink_data.html
This list of data sources, created by Dr. Joseph Kerski of ESRI (formerly with the U.S. Geological Survey), is a good resource to find data to build GIS projects.

www.esri.com/ourworldgiseducation
Web site for *Our World GIS Education, Level 4, Making Spatial Decisions Using GIS.*

ESRI Press Books

A to Z GIS: An Illustrated Dictionary of Geographic Information Systems. A great guide to the lexicon of GIS.

ArcGIS 9, Understanding Map Projections. This digital book is an excellent introduction to the details of map projections and geographic transformations.

GIS Tutorial, Second Edition. This workbook combines ArcGIS tutorials and self-study exercises that start with the basics and progress to more difficult functionality.

Video

What is GIS?
This video clip included on your DVD in the General Documents folder looks at the many uses of GIS software to create maps, analyze data, and make better decisions.

ArcMap toolbar quick reference

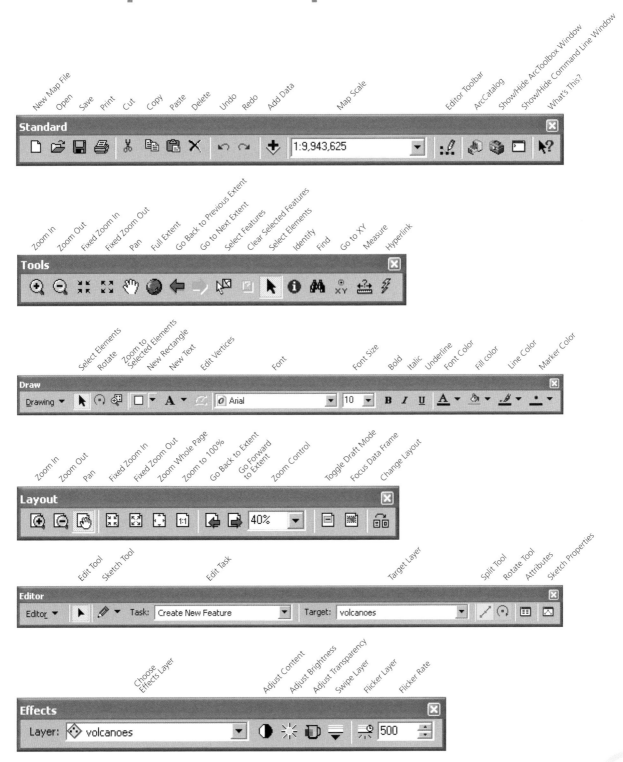

Extensions toolbar quick reference

ArcGIS Network Analyst Extension

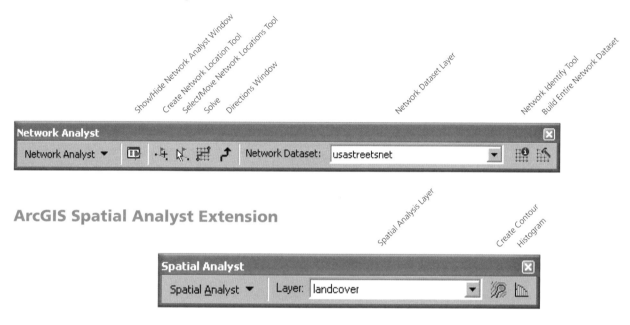

ArcGIS Spatial Analyst Extension

ArcGIS 3D Analyst Extension and ArcScene

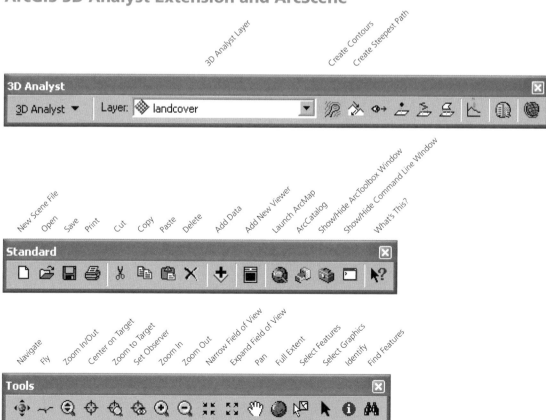

References and photo credits

References (module 2)

Cohen, Joel. E. 2003. Human population: The next half century. *Science*. (November 14). Vol. 302. No. 5648, pp.1172–175.

United Nations Population Fund. 2007. *State of World Population 2007. Unleashing the Potential of Urban Growth.* http://www.unfpa.org/swp/2007/english/introduction.html.

Photo credits

Module 1—U.S. Environmental Protection Agency

Module 2—Kent Knudson/PhotoLink/PhotoDisc/Getty Images

Module 3—Mark Downey/PhotoDisc/Getty Images

Module 4—C. Lee/PhotoLink/PhotoDisc/Getty Images

Module 5—F. Schussler/PhotoLink/PhotoDisc/Getty Images

Data sources

**Module 1, Project 1 - \OurWorld4\student\Module1\Project1\data\Springfield.gdb
data sources include:**

\additional_layers\bldg feature class, courtesy of the County of Fairfax, Virginia.
\additional_layers\counties feature class, from ESRI Data & Maps 2006, courtesy of U.S. Census.
\additional_layers\gschools feature class, from ESRI Data & Maps 2006, courtesy of USGS – GNIS.
\additional_layers\route1 feature class, from ESRI Data & Maps 2006, courtesy of USGS – GNIS.
\additional_layers\route2 feature class, from ESRI Data & Maps 2006, courtesy of USGS – GNIS.
\additional_layers\route3 feature class, from ESRI Data & Maps 2006, courtesy of USGS – GNIS.
\network\usastreets feature class, from ESRI ArcGIS StreetMap USA, courtesy of Tele Atlas.
\network\usastreetsnet feature class, from ESRI ArcGIS StreetMap USA, courtesy of Tele Atlas.
\network\usastreetsnet_Junctions feature class, from ESRI ArcGIS StreetMap USA, courtesy of Tele Atlas.
\aerial\Band_1 feature class, data available from U.S. Geological Survey, EROS Data Center, Sioux Falls, SD.
\aerial\Band_2 feature class, data available from U.S. Geological Survey, EROS Data Center, Sioux Falls, SD.
\aerial\Band_3 feature class, data available from U.S. Geological Survey, EROS Data Center, Sioux Falls, SD.

**Module 1, Project 2 - \OurWorld4\student\Module1\Project2\data\Mecklenburg.gdb
data sources include:**

\AdditionalLayers\blkgrp feature class, from ESRI Data & Maps 2006, courtesy of Tele Atlas and U.S. Census.
\AdditionalLayers\county feature class, from ESRI Data & Maps 2006, courtesy of U.S. Census.
\AdditionalLayers\detour1stops feature class, from ESRI Data & Maps 2006, courtesy of USGS – GNIS.
\AdditionalLayers\detour2stops feature class, from ESRI Data & Maps 2006, courtesy of USGS – GNIS.
\AdditionalLayers\detour3stops feature class, from ESRI Data & Maps 2006, courtesy of USGS – GNIS.
\AdditionalLayers\detour4stops feature class, from ESRI Data & Maps 2006, courtesy of USGS – GNIS.
\AdditionalLayers\detour5stops feature class, from ESRI Data & Maps 2006, courtesy of USGS – GNIS.
\AdditionalLayers\gschools feature class, from ESRI Data & Maps 2006, courtesy of USGS – GNIS.
\Network\Network_ND feature class, from ESRI ArcGIS StreetMap USA, courtesy of Tele Atlas.
\Network\Network_ND_Junctions feature class, from ESRI ArcGIS StreetMap USA, courtesy of Tele Atlas.
\Network\usastreets feature class, from ESRI ArcGIS StreetMap USA, courtesy of Tele Atlas.
\aerial\Band_1 feature class, data available from U.S. Geological Survey, EROS Data Center, Sioux Falls, SD.
\aerial\Band_2 feature class, data available from U.S. Geological Survey, EROS Data Center, Sioux Falls, SD.
\aerial\Band_3 feature class, data available from U.S. Geological Survey, EROS Data Center, Sioux Falls, SD.

**Module 2, Project 1 - \OurWorld4\student\Module2\Project1\data\Chicago.gdb
data sources include:**

\chicago feature class from ESRI Data & Maps 2006 courtesy of Tele Atlas.
\county feature class from ESRI Data & Maps 2006, courtesy of Tele Atlas and U.S. Census.
\tracts_00 feature class from ESRI Data & Maps 2006, courtesy of U.S. Census.
\tracts_90 feature class from ESRI Data & Maps 1999.
\dt_dec_2000_sf4_u_data001_1 data , courtesy of U.S. Census.
\dt_dec_2000_sf4_u_geo data, courtesy of U.S. Census.

Module 2, Project 2 - \OurWorld4\student\Module2\Project2\data\DC.gdb data sources include:

\dc feature class from ESRI Data & Maps, courtesy of Tele Atlas and U.S. Census.
\dtl_water feature class from ESRI Data & Maps 2006, courtesy of USGS.
\mjr_hwys feature class from ESRI Data & Maps 2006, courtesy of ESRI.
\tracts_00 feature class from ESRI Data & Maps 2006, courtesy of U.S. Census.
\tracts_90 feature class from ESRI Data & Maps 1999.
\dt_dec_2000_sf3_u_data1 data, courtesy of U.S. Census.
\dt_dec_2000_sf3_u_geo data, courtesy of U.S. Census.

Module 3, Project 1 -\OurWorld4\student\Module3\Project1\data\Houston.gdb data sources include:

\blkgrp feature class from ESRI Data & Maps 2006, courtesy of U.S. Census.
\highways feature class from ESRI Data & Maps 2006, courtesy of ESRI.
\houston feature class, courtesy of the Houston Police Department.
\main_usa_sts feature class from ESRI Data & Maps 2006, courtesy of Tele Atlas.
\places feature class from ESRI Data & Maps 2006, courtesy of U.S. Census.
\schools feature class from ESRI Data & Maps 2006, courtesy of USGS – GNIS.
\usa_sts feature class from ESRI Data & Maps 2006, courtesy of ESRI.
\aug06 data courtesy of the City of Houston.
\police_stations courtesy of the City of Houston.

Module 3, Project 2 - \OurWorld4\student\Module3\Project2\data\Lincoln.gdb data sources include:

\aug_06 feature class courtesy of the City of Houston.
\blkgrp feature class from ESRI Data & Maps 2006, courtesy of U.S. Census.
\lincoln feature class courtesy of the Lincoln Police Department.
\places feature class from ESRI Data & Maps 2006, courtesy of U.S. Census.
\usa_streets from ESRI ArcGIS StreetMap USA, courtesy of Tele Atlas.
\police_stations data, courtesy of the Lincoln Police Department.
\Streets feature class from ESRI Data & Maps 2006, courtesy of ESRI.
\UCR CODES courtesy of the Lincoln Police Department.

Module 4, Project 1 -\OurWorld4\student\Module4\Project1\data\Katrina.gdb data sources include:

\airports feature class, from ESRI Data and Maps, courtesy of Tele Atlas.
\airports feature class, courtesy of the National Atlas of the United States, the Bureau of Transportation Statistics, USGS, The Federal Aviation Administration, and the U.S. Department of Transportation.
\churches feature class from ESRI Data & Maps 2006, courtesy of USGS – GNIS.
\counties feature class data available from U.S. Geological Survey, EROS Data Center, Sioux Falls, SD.
\elev feature class data available from U.S. Geological Survey, EROS Data Center, Sioux Falls, SD.
\hospitals feature class from ESRI Data & Maps 2006, courtesy of USGS – GNIS.
\islands feature class data available from U.S. Geological Survey, EROS Data Center, Sioux Falls, SD.
\landcover feature class data available from U.S. Geological Survey, EROS Data Center, Sioux Falls, SD.
\places feature class from ESRI Data & Maps 2006, courtesy of USGS – GNIS.
\railroads feature class from ESRI Data & Maps 2006, courtesy of U.S. Bureau of Transportation Statistics.
\rivers feature class from ESRI Data & Maps 2006, courtesy of USGS.
\usa_streets feature class from ESRI Data & Maps 2006, courtesy of ESRI.
\water feature class from ESRI Data & Maps 2006, courtesy of USGS.

Module 4, Project 2 - \OurWorld4\student\Module4\Project2\data\Wilma.gdb data sources include:

\airports feature class, from ESRI Data and Maps, courtesy of Tele Atlas.

\airports feature class, courtesy of the National Atlas of the United States, the Bureau of Transportation Statistics, USGS, The Federal Aviation Administration, and the U.S. Department of Transportation.

\elev feature class data available from U.S. Geological Survey, EROS Data Center, Sioux Falls, SD.

\gchurch feature class from ESRI Data & Maps 2006, courtesy of USGS – GNIS.

\ghospitals feature class from ESRI Data & Maps 2006, courtesy of USGS – GNIS.

\gschools feature class from ESRI Data & Maps 2006, courtesy of USGS – GNIS.

\keywest feature class derived from ESRI Data & Maps 2006, courtesy of Tele Atlas and U.S. Census.

\landcover feature class data available from U.S. Geological Survey, EROS Data Center, Sioux Falls, SD.

\places feature class from ESRI Data & Maps 2006, courtesy of USGS – GNIS.

\usa_streets feature class from ESRI Data & Maps 2006, courtesy of ESRI.

Module 5, Project 1 - \OurWorld4\student\Module5\Project1\data\Location.gdb data sources include:

\county feature class from ESRI Data & Maps 2006, courtesy of U.S. Census.

\fedland feature class from ESRI Data & Maps 2006, courtesy of The National Atlas of the United States.

\hospitals feature class from ESRI Data & Maps 2006, courtesy of USGS – GNIS.

\places feature class from ESRI Data & Maps 2006, courtesy of USGS – GNIS.

\schools feature class from ESRI Data & Maps 2006, courtesy of USGS – GNIS.

\sel_tracts feature class from ESRI Data & Maps 2006, courtesy of U.S. Census.

\tracts feature class from ESRI Data & Maps 2006, courtesy of U.S. Census.

\dt_dec_2000_sf3_u_data1 data, courtesy of U.S. Census.

\dt_dec_2000_sf3_u_geo data, courtesy of U.S. Census.

Module 5, Project 2 - \OurWorld4\student\Module5\Project2\data\Ohio.gdb data sources include:

\counties feature class from ESRI Data & Maps 2006, courtesy of U.S. Census.

\places feature class from ESRI Data & Maps 2006, courtesy of USGS – GNIS.

\schools feature class from ESRI Data & Maps 2006, courtesy of USGS – GNIS.

\tracts feature class from ESRI Data & Maps 2006, courtesy of U.S. Census.

Data license agreement

Important: Read carefully before opening the sealed media package

Environmental Systems Research Institute, Inc. (ESRI), is willing to license the enclosed data and related materials to you only upon the condition that you accept all of the terms and conditions contained in this license agreement. Please read the terms and conditions carefully before opening the sealed media package. By opening the sealed media package, you are indicating your acceptance of the ESRI License Agreement. If you do not agree to the terms and conditions as stated, then ESRI is unwilling to license the data and related materials to you. In such event, you should return the media package with the seal unbroken and all other components to ESRI.

ESRI License Agreement

This is a license agreement, and not an agreement for sale, between you (Licensee) and Environmental Systems Research Institute, Inc. (ESRI). This ESRI License Agreement (Agreement) gives Licensee certain limited rights to use the data and related materials (Data and Related Materials). All rights not specifically granted in this Agreement are reserved to ESRI and its Licensors.

Reservation of Ownership and Grant of License: ESRI and its Licensors retain exclusive rights, title, and ownership to the copy of the Data and Related Materials licensed under this Agreement and, hereby, grant to Licensee a personal, nonexclusive, nontransferable, royalty-free, worldwide license to use the Data and Related Materials based on the terms and conditions of this Agreement. Licensee agrees to use reasonable effort to protect the Data and Related Materials from unauthorized use, reproduction, distribution, or publication.

Proprietary Rights and Copyright: Licensee acknowledges that the Data and Related Materials are proprietary and confidential property of ESRI and its Licensors and are protected by United States copyright laws and applicable international copyright treaties and/or conventions.

Permitted Uses: Licensee may install the Data and Related Materials onto permanent storage device(s) for Licensee's own internal use.

Licensee may make only one (1) copy of the original Data and Related Materials for archival purposes during the term of this Agreement unless the right to make additional copies is granted to Licensee in writing by ESRI.

Licensee may internally use the Data and Related Materials provided by ESRI for the stated purpose of GIS training and education.

Uses Not Permitted: Licensee shall not sell, rent, lease, sublicense, lend, assign, time-share, or transfer, in whole or in part, or provide unlicensed Third Parties access to the Data and Related Materials or portions of the Data and Related Materials, any updates, or Licensee's rights under this Agreement.

175

Licensee shall not remove or obscure any copyright or trademark notices of ESRI or its Licensors.

Term and Termination: The license granted to Licensee by this Agreement shall commence upon the acceptance of this Agreement and shall continue until such time that Licensee elects in writing to discontinue use of the Data or Related Materials and terminates this Agreement. The Agreement shall automatically terminate without notice if Licensee fails to comply with any provision of this Agreement. Licensee shall then return to ESRI the Data and Related Materials. The parties hereby agree that all provisions that operate to protect the rights of ESRI and its Licensors shall remain in force should breach occur.

Disclaimer of Warranty: The Data and Related Materials contained herein are provided "as-is," without warranty of any kind, either express or implied, including, but not limited to, the implied warranties of merchantability, fitness for a particular purpose, or noninfringement. ESRI does not warrant that the Data and Related Materials will meet Licensee's needs or expectations, that the use of the Data and Related Materials will be uninterrupted, or that all nonconformities, defects, or errors can or will be corrected. ESRI is not inviting reliance on the Data or Related Materials for commercial planning or analysis purposes, and Licensee should always check actual data.

Data Disclaimer: The Data used herein has been derived from actual spatial or tabular information. In some cases, ESRI has manipulated and applied certain assumptions, analyses, and opinions to the Data solely for educational training purposes. Assumptions, analyses, opinions applied, and actual outcomes may vary. Again, ESRI is not inviting reliance on this Data, and the Licensee should always verify actual Data and exercise their own professional judgment when interpreting any outcomes.

Limitation of Liability: ESRI shall not be liable for direct, indirect, special, incidental, or consequential damages related to Licensee's use of the Data and Related Materials, even if ESRI is advised of the possibility of such damage.

No Implied Waivers: No failure or delay by ESRI or its Licensors in enforcing any right or remedy under this Agreement shall be construed as a waiver of any future or other exercise of such right or remedy by ESRI or its Licensors.

Order for Precedence: Any conflict between the terms of this Agreement and any FAR, DFAR, purchase order, or other terms shall be resolved in favor of the terms expressed in this Agreement, subject to the government's minimum rights unless agreed otherwise.

Export Regulation: Licensee acknowledges that this Agreement and the performance thereof are subject to compliance with any and all applicable United States laws, regulations, or orders relating to the export of data thereto. Licensee agrees to comply with all laws, regulations, and orders of the United States in regard to any export of such technical data.

Severability: If any provision(s) of this Agreement shall be held to be invalid, illegal, or unenforceable by a court or other tribunal of competent jurisdiction, the validity, legality, and enforceability of the remaining provisions shall not in any way be affected or impaired thereby.

Governing Law: This Agreement, entered into in the County of San Bernardino, shall be construed and enforced in accordance with and be governed by the laws of the United States of America and the State of California without reference to conflict of laws principles. The parties hereby consent to the personal jurisdiction of the courts of this county and waive their rights to change venue.

Entire Agreement: The parties agree that this Agreement constitutes the sole and entire agreement of the parties as to the matter set forth herein and supersedes any previous agreements, understandings, and arrangements between the parties relating hereto.

Installing the data and resources

Making Spatial Decisions Using GIS includes two DVDs at the back of the book. Look for the one labeled Student Data and resources. This DVD contains the GIS data and other documents you will need to complete the projects.

Installation of the Student Data and resources DVD requires approximately 841 megabytes of disk space.

Follow the steps below to install the files. Do not copy the files directly from the DVD to your hard drive. A direct file copy does not remove write-protection from the files, and this causes data editing steps in the projects not to work.

1. Put the DVD in your computer's DVD drive. A window like the one below will appear.

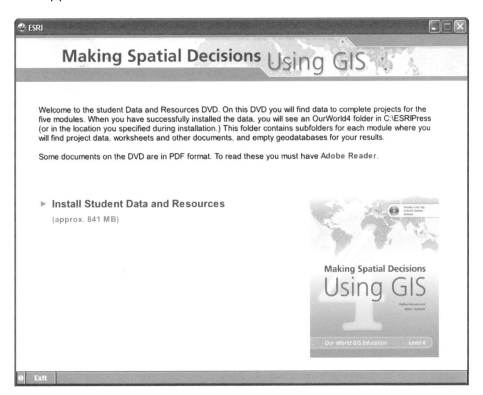

2. Read the welcome, then click the Install Student Data and Resources link. This launches the InstallShield Wizard.

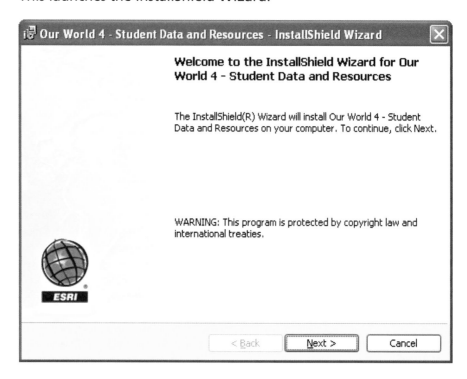

3. Click Next. Read and accept the license agreement terms, then click Next.

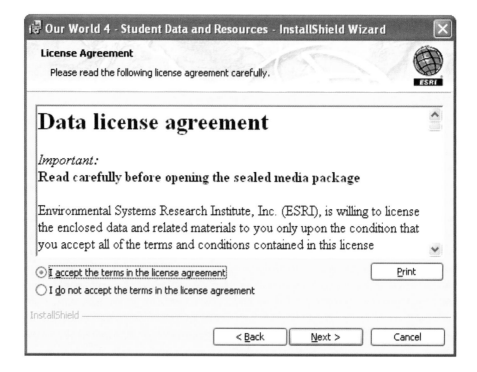

4. Accept the default installation folder or click Change and navigate to the drive or folder location where you want to install the data. Please make a note of where you install the data.

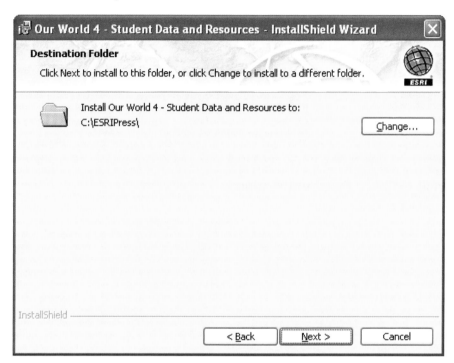

5. Click Next. The installation will take a few moments. When the installation is complete, you will see the following message:

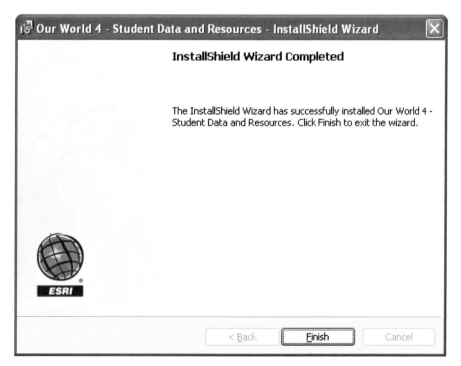

6. Click Finish. The student data is installed on your computer in a folder called OurWorld4.

If you have a licensed copy of ArcGIS Desktop 9 (ArcView, ArcEditor, or ArcInfo license) installed on your computer, you are ready to start Making Spatial Decisions Using ArcGIS. Otherwise, follow the Installing the software instructions to install and register the trial software.

Uninstalling the data and resources

To uninstall the data and resources from your computer, open your operating system's control panel and double-click the Add/Remove Programs icon. In the Add/Remove Programs dialog box, select the following entry and follow the prompts to remove it:

OurWorld4 - Student Data and Resources

Installing and registering the trial software

The ArcGIS software included on this DVD is intended for educational purposes only. Once installed and registered, the software will run for 180 days. The software cannot be reinstalled nor can the time limit be extended. It is recommended that you uninstall this software when it expires.

System requirements

Before installing the ArcGIS Desktop 9.2 software, make sure your computer meets these system requirements:

- Microsoft Windows XP, Windows 2000 or Windows Vista operating system
- Disk space 1.2 GB
- RAM 1 GB minimum
- DVD drive (required for installation)

Note for users of Windows Vista

Service Pack 4 for ArcGIS 9.2 is required for Windows Vista support. There are some additional issues that you should be aware of before working with ArcGIS 9.2 on Windows Vista. Please visit this book's Web site (www.esri.com/ourworldgiseducation) for more information.

Install the software

Follow the steps below to install the software.

1. Put the software DVD in your computer's DVD drive. A splash screen will appear.

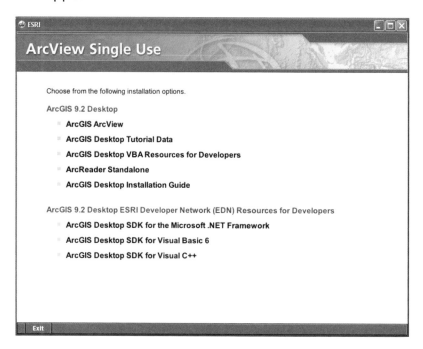

2. Click the ArcGIS ArcView installation option. On the Startup window, click Install ArcGIS Desktop. This will launch the Setup wizard.

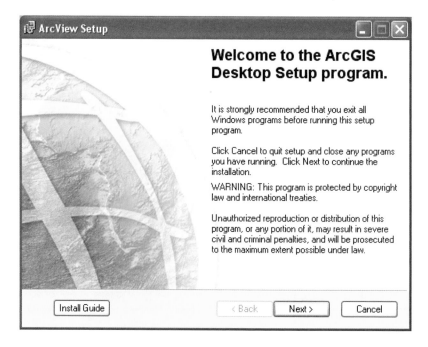

3. Read the Welcome, then click Next.

4. Read the license agreement. Click "I accept the license agreement" and click Next.

5. The default installation type is Typical. You must choose the Complete install, which will add extension products that are used in the book. Click the button next to Complete.

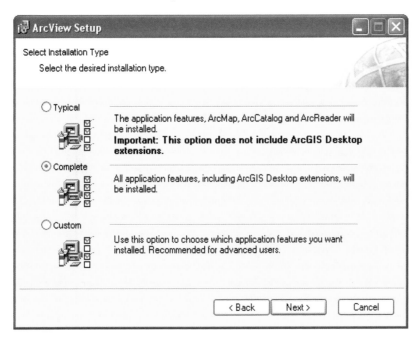

6. Click Next. Accept the default installation folder or click Browse and navigate to the drive or folder location where you want to install the software.

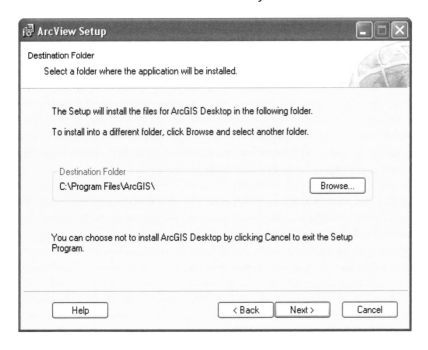

183

7. Click Next. Accept the default installation folder or navigate to the drive or folder where you want to install Python, a scripting language used by some ArcGIS geoprocessing functions. (You won't see this panel if you already have Python installed.) Click Next.

8. The installation paths for ArcGIS and Python are confirmed. Click Next. The software will take several minutes to install on your computer. When the installation is finished, you will see the following message:

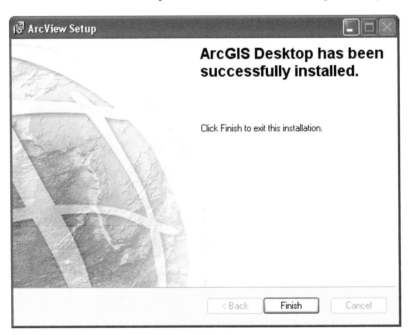

9. Click Finish.

Register the software

10. Locate your registration code on the software DVD jacket in the back of the book.

11. On the next panel, click Register Now and select the desired registration option. Be sure to register the three extensions used in this book (Network Analyst, Spatial Analyst, and 3D Analyst).

- *If you register automatically using the Internet, be sure to fill in the Organization field with a complete name; do not use an acronym or abbreviation or leave it blank. If you receive a message indicating a problem, contact ESRI Customer Service at 888-377-4575 to resolve it. Once the registration is complete you can start using ArcGIS Desktop.*

- *If you register manually, you will receive an authorization file in a *.esu9 format. Save this file to your computer. Open the Registration Wizard from the Desktop administrator and finish the registration process. Browse to the saved authorization file to complete the registration.*

Download and install the latest Service Pack

ESRI periodically releases software updates and corrections called service packs. The projects in this book require a minimum of ArcGIS 9.2, Service Pack 3 for all instructions to work properly. The following steps will guide you to download the latest service pack from the Internet and install it on your computer. *Note: You must have ArcGIS 9.2 installed and registered before you install the service pack.*

1. Connect your computer to the Internet and browse to http://support.esri.com.

2. Click the Downloads tab at the top of the page, and then click Patches and Service Packs.

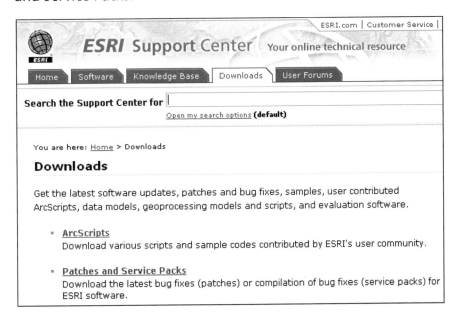

3. Scroll down the list and click ArcView.

- ArcPad StreetMap (1 file)

- ArcReader (16 files)

- ArcSDE *(9.1 and older)* (55 files)

- ArcView (51 files)

- ArcView 3.x (42 files)

- ArcWeb Services APIs (28 files)

4. Click the link for the latest ArcGIS 9.2 service pack (Service Pack 4 was the latest one available when this book went to press.)

> 📄 <u>ArcGIS 9.2 Service Pack 4</u>
> November 16, 2007 - SERVICE PACK
> This Service Pack contains performance improvements and maintenance fixes. Please download and install this required Service Pack at your earliest convenience.

5. Scroll down to the Installation Steps section. You will need to download the ArcView 9.2 Evaluation Edition files if you installed the trial software that comes with this book. (If you are using a fully licensed version of ArcGIS Desktop, download the ArcGIS Desktop (ArcView, ArcEditor, ArcInfo) files instead.) Click the msp link to save the files to your computer.

> **ArcView 9.2 Evaluation Edition**
> <u>ArcGISEvalEdition92sp4.msp</u>   175 MB

6. Close your Internet browser. In your operating system's file browser, navigate to the saved msp file. Double click the msp file to start the install process. When Setup starts, follow the instructions on your screen.

If you have questions or encounter problems during the installation process, or while using this book, please use the resources listed below. (ESRI Support Services does not answer questions regarding the ArcGIS 9 trial software DVD, the student data and resources, or the contents of the book itself.)

To resolve problems with the trial software or exercise data, or to report mistakes in the book, send and email to ESRI workbook support at learngis@esri.com.

To stay informed about exercise updates, frequently asked questions, and errata, visit the book's Web page at www.esri.com/ourworldgiseducation.

Uninstalling the software

To uninstall the software from your computer, open your operating system's control panel and double-click the Add/Remove Programs icon. In the Add/Remove Programs dialog box, select the following entry and follow the prompts to remove it:

ArcGIS Desktop